HARVARD HISTORICAL STUDIES

Published under the direction
of the Department of History
from the income of the
Paul Revere Frothingham Bequest

Volume XCIX

Frontispiece. *Anne of Brittany as the Figure of Justice*, by Michel Colombe. Tomb of the Dukes of Brittany, Cathedral of Nantes.

# Judicial Reform in France
# before the Revolution of 1789

## John A. Carey

Harvard University Press
Cambridge, Massachusetts
and London, England
1981

Library of Congress Cataloging in Publication Data

Carey, John A., 1949–
   Judicial reform in France before the Revolution of 1789.

   (Harvard historical studies; v. 99)
   Bibliography: p.
   Includes index.
   1. Courts—France—History. I. Title. II. Series.
Law                  347.44                    81-6463
ISBN 0-674-48878-4        344.407              AACR2

TO MY FATHER
AND TO THE MEMORY OF MY MOTHER

# Acknowledgments

For their help and encouragement with this work I wish to thank Professor Patrice L.-R. Higonnet and Professor Franklin L. Ford of the Department of History at Harvard University.

To many others I am also indebted. I thank my sister for her help, which included obtaining some of the illustrations. I am grateful to my uncle and aunt, Professor and Mrs. L. A. Bordwell, for their interest in my project. For inviting me to discuss my project and for sharing with me their thoughts on it, I thank Dr. Yvette Sheahan Kirby, Professor Matthew Ramsey, and the other members of the French History Study Group at Harvard. During my final revision of this work, the people at The Pioneer Group, Inc., added their good wishes and counsel, and I thank them, too.

For speeding my work along and providing me with many useful suggestions, I thank Professor John L. Clive, editor of the Harvard Historical Studies series, Mrs. Madeleine Gleason, and the editorial staff at the Harvard University Press. Ms. Celia Shneider has my gratitude for typing the final draft of the text, and Mr. Ulf Andersen of Paris, France, has my thanks for taking the picture of L'Hospital's tomb.

I am grateful to the Harvard Center for European Studies for a travel grant in the summer of 1974. For the gift of a microfilm reader, I thank the General Microfilm Company of Cambridge, Massachusetts. Finally I thank, for their friendly, expert, and generous assistance, the librarians and archivists of Harvard and Oxford universities; the Library of Congress; the Bibliothèque publique de la ville de Neuchâtel (Switzerland); the Bibliothèque Nationale, Archives Nationales, and Bibliothèque Sainte-Geneviève; the Institut de France; the Archives municipales de la Ville de Rennes; the Université de Besançon; and the Archives départementales de l'Aisne, de l'Allier, de l'Aude, de la Charente-Maritime, de la Côte-d'Or, de la Dordogne, de la Drôme, de la Haute-Saône, de l'Hérault, d'Ille-et-Vilaine, du Lot, de la Marne, de Midi-Pyrénées et de la

Haute-Garonne, des Pyrénées-Atlantiques, des Pyrénées-Orientales, de la Sarthe, de la Somme, du Var, and de l'Yonne.

The departmental archivists enabled me to complete research that I could not conduct in person. Every one with whom I corresponded was enormously obliging. Some answered questions for me; several provided me with microfilm of many hundreds of pages of documents. All were indispensable to me, and I must thank them again.

My greatest debts I acknowledge in the dedication.

Translations are mine unless otherwise noted, and all book titles are given in their original spelling.

Archives départementales are abbreviated throughout the book as A.D.

# Contents

# Illustrations

# Introduction

This is a study of judicial reform in France before the 1789 revolution, of its failure, and of the consequences of that failure. From a longer view, this is also a study of reform itself and its different meanings. The court reforms that the king's ministers tried between the 1720s and 1788 were mutations in royal legislation, resulting, this study argues, from a new and distinctive influence on the ministers. That influence was a concept of reform that had developed during the seventeenth century. The concept still exists. With its formulation came the ambiguity in the word *reform* that continues to jumble the thought, and unfortunately also the actions, of many who use that word. For the new idea of reform did not replace, but rather intertwined itself with, the old one in unsustainable disagreement. The study of judicial reform in France will thus reveal an instance of the difficulties that reformers yet find.

## Traditional and Modern Reform

Until the early seventeenth century, Frenchmen used the verb *réformer* only in its classical sense, that is, according to the meanings of the Latin word, *reformare,* from which it was derived: to shape again or remold, to alter or amend, to restore or reestablish. Beginning with Mathurin Régnier, who satirized precise conformity to classical standards, and continuing with Descartes, Pascal, and the funeral orator and moralist Esprit-Valentin Fléchier, Frenchmen added another meaning to the word: to change radically in view of ameliorating morally or intellectually.[1] Not only had *reformare* never been so defined, but classical Latin may never have had an equivalent of "radical reform."[2]

To illustrate the difference between the older and newer meanings of *reform,* consider a person who finds a fork with a bent tine. If he were a classical or "traditional" reformer, he would either bend back the tine to restore the fork to its original shape or melt down the fork and recast it into that shape. The "modern" reformer would note the bent tine and ask himself whether it might not be symptomatic of something radically wrong with the fork, perhaps with respect to its design or the metal from which it was made—something that made the fork susceptible to getting its tines bent. He might, therefore, set the fork aside, start all over again with a new design or a different metal, and make another fork whose prongs he did not think would be liable ever to bend. Thus would he reform the fork.

Traditional reform required historical or legal precedent; modern reform, theoretical justification. As early physicians sought to cure a patient by rebalancing the four vital fluids in his body, so traditional reformers tried to correct what had gone wrong but gave no thought to creating anew. They were concerned only with readjusting institutions or putting them back into their historical equilibrium. Modern reformers, by contrast, looked outside of history. They took their models for reform from their imagination.

Traditional and modern reform cannot be achieved simultaneously. To effect them both would be a physical impossibility similar to repairing and replacing the foundation of a house at the same time. One has to decide which one wants to do.

As approaches to change, both traditional and modern reform may be criticized. At their least perceptive, traditional reformers attempted to reestablish what had been without considering why it no longer was. At their shrewdest, they still tried to restore institutions as they had been but to provide better this time for their survival. Even at their shrewdest, however, they did not comprehend that historical situations are unique and thus cannot be re-created.

Modern reformers, too, met difficult problems in changing institutions successfully. The problems seemed so difficult, indeed, that Descartes, one of the first people to use the word *reform* in its modern sense, did not think that one could profitably address them at all. He accompanied his new definition of *reform* with a strict injunction against applying it to programs for reforming the state. It is well to keep in mind the full title of his *Discourse Concerning the Method for Conducting One's Reason Well and for Seeking the Truth in the Sciences* (1637). Descartes thought his method useful in the analysis of things logically and clearly explicable. He thought it not at all helpful in finding and understanding the often illogical and vague reasons for the establishment of particular social and political institutions, let alone in determining what an improvement on those institutions would be. He applied his method to optics, physics, medicine, and astronomy, but never to the order of the state.

States had their imperfections, in the view of Descartes, but custom had tempered these imperfections, even "avoided or corrected" imperfections that no legislator could have foreseen, so that they were "almost always more endurable than their changes" would have been. He did suspect, for instance, that "since the multiplicity of laws often furnishes excuses for vices . . . a state is better regulated when it has only a very few laws that are observed very strictly." But, believing that one should act on the basis of knowledge, not suspicion, he did not assert that one should reform the laws if they were many.[3]

In Descartes' view, one should not think about that which one cannot know with mathematical certainty, about that of which one can never know the truth but only the possibilities. In such an area of uncertainty, one should accept the pertinent moderate opinion and turn one's attention elsewhere. Because the state and its laws have been imperceptibly and hence unknowably modified by custom, Descartes did not presume to investigate them. He urged others not to investigate them either. "I should not know at all how to approve," he said, "of those persons of unaccountable and restless temperament who, being called neither by their birth nor by their fortune to the management of public affairs, do not fail always to imagine some new reform. And if I thought that there had been the least thing in this work on the basis of which one could have suspected me of this folly, I should be very sorry for having allowed this work to be published."[4]

Barely thirty years later, however, jurists and political thinkers, disregarding Descartes' warning, began applying the methods of scientific inquiry indiscriminately. These methods were generalized and popularized by Fontenelle and others; and well into the eighteenth century, and beyond, people fancied themselves able to use them profitably in all areas of their lives. In 1719, the chancellor of France, Henri-François d'Aguesseau, wrote to his son:

Philosophy and mathematics have this advantage, that, as they exercise the mind on the most abstract and subtle matters, those who have once been able to surmount the difficulties in them no longer find anything difficult in the other sciences; and the method in which they are trained, being as a universal instrument that applies itself equally to all sorts of subjects, there is none of them that they do not know how to bring back to its first principles and that they are not capable of treating in a superior manner.[5]

D'Aguesseau's letter would have distressed Descartes. The Revolution of 1789, which may be said to have carried to an extreme the application "to all sorts of subjects" of scientific methods, then styled common sense, would have confirmed his worst anxieties. But no one can control how a word will be used, and the new meaning that Descartes and other seventeenth-century philosophers had restricted to moral and intellectual reform, other Frenchmen soon applied to political and institutional reform as well.

*The Confusion of Traditional and Modern Reform in the Eighteenth Century*

Modern reform by no means immediately displaced traditional reform. The reforming chancellors and keepers of the seals of eighteenth-century France usually claimed, indeed, that they were but carrying forward the traditional reforms attempted by their predecessors. The example of these earlier reformers, they said, inspired, sustained, and justified them. "My duties were laid out for me," said Chancellor Maupeou, in defending his actions during 1771–1774, "by the most enlightened men who have filled the office that I have the honor to occupy. Let one bring together the monuments that remain to us of the Oliviers, of the L'Hospitals, of the d'Aguesseaus, one will find everywhere among them my principles; and these principles, developed with even more strength and energy, one will find in all the public depositories, in all the endorsed works of the parlements and the sovereign authority."[6] During discussions on judicial reform in 1784, when he was *président à mortier* of the Parlement of Paris, Chrétien-François II de Lamoignon took heart from a harangue that L'Hospital had delivered to the Parlement of Rouen in 1563. "This event struck me so much," said Lamoignon, "that I chose it immediately to have before my eyes at all times; and it is to its repeated reading that I owe the total accomplishment of the work that I set out for myself of determining a plan for reform, without which the bar cannot subsist nor honest men continue to wear a robe that becomes for them from day to day a more insupportable burden."[7]

D'Aguesseau, for his part, cited the pioneering efforts of Brisson
during the reign of Henry III at collecting and arranging the ordonnances of the French kings after the form of the Code of Justinian
and the work at codification and the reform of civil and criminal
procedure undertaken during the reign of Louis XIV as the starting
points for his own work.[8] With respect to the présidiaux, on which
he concentrated so much of his attention, the chancellor claimed to
be returning the courts to the way they had been—or to the way
they should have been had not financial motives interfered—when
created by Henry II in 1552. In proposing to allow the courts final
jurisdiction over civil suits in which more was at stake, the chancellor argued that he would have been merely restoring to the présidiaux the civil jurisdictions that they had had before monetary inflation reduced their intended extent.[9]

But d'Aguesseau, Maupeou, and Lamoignon also said, on occasion, that they were innovating. To a larger extent than they knew,
they were correct, for modern reform had occurred right alongside
traditional reform. Though the three officials followed precedents
for reform set during the Renaissance, their reforms had a wholly
different character. Though they made use for the most part of existing institutions, their reforms, or at least some of them, would
have changed the institutions beyond recognition. Difficulties arose
from the crown's seeming inability to distinguish between restoring
institutions and turning them inside out. When it set out to restore
them it was inattentive to their nature and inadvertently wrecked
them. When it intended to turn them inside out, it did not do all
that was required and succeeded only in fortifying them in their customary practices. Unmindful of the implications of its reforms, and
also of what would remain if the reforms collapsed, the crown, at its
worst, brusquely, even violently, changed the rules and then
changed them back again without changing the players and without
having any thoughtful reasons for doing either.

The crown's failure at reform made the Revolution possible, and
so it is important to understand why the failure occurred. By way of
explanation, historians have often pointed out that political, social,
and economic pressures limited what the crown could do. When the
crown made reforms, these pressures forced it to rescind them. What
historians of the field have not sufficiently appreciated, however, is
the inherent ambiguity in the crown's reforms. For the crown was

reforming in two ways during the eighteenth century, one traditional, the other modern. The incompatibility and friction between the two approaches, which went largely unnoticed until the 1770s, made all the crown's reforming steps even more halting, and ultimately disastrous, than reaction alone could have made them. The moral and institutional wreckage from the most confused attempt at reform during the Old Regime, that of Chancellor Maupeou, blocked further reform before the Revolution while making reform more necessary than ever and stimulating increased concern about it. As a result of the Maupeou years, the incompatibility of traditional with modern reform was first seen.

The dialogue on court reform during the Old Regime was conducted by small numbers of people. Nearly all were lawyers and judges, or royal ministers who were usually former lawyers or judges. The exceptional works on law courts published outside legal and governmental circles tended either to reflect the views expressed in those circles or to complain, in the way that was common during the Middle Ages and is still common today, about pettifoggery, judicial ignorance, slow and expensive litigation, and cumbersomely formal court proceedings.

Works on court reform also appeared in clusters, usually in periods when the crown was contemplating or attempting reform. Almost all of the lawyers and judges who left a record of their thoughts on court reform were responding to a survey of them or to a legislative initiative by the crown.

Broader participation might be found in other Old Regime dialogues on reform, such as those on financial, ecclesiastical, military, agricultural, municipal, educational, moral, and linguistic reform. The discussion on judicial reform is presented here because it was continual and hence its development may be shown and explained by relating it to the course of French history. Frenchmen evidently attached great importance to judicial reform, as indicated by the frequency of their calls for it in the *cahiers de doléances* that they drew up for the Estates-General.

Judicial reform refers here to reform of the courts that regularly tried a broad range of civil and criminal cases—namely, the parlements, the présidiaux, bailliages, and sénéchaussées, and the seignorial courts. All types of changes proposed in these courts between the sixteenth and eighteenth centuries will be considered. These changes or reforms may be classified as: (1) procedural; (2) organizational (internal, appellate, or jurisdictional); (3) disciplinary or professional; (4) structural (changes in fundamental characteristics of the court system—notably, the venality and heritability of judicial offices and the judges' collection of *épices,* or gifts, fees, and other emoluments from litigants to supplement their *gages,* or official interest income); and (5) supportive (security-supportive laws to guard judicial officers, particularly the minor officials of the courts, against any who might try, through bribes, threats, or violence, to keep them from going about their work; and, especially when urged on the crown by the judges themselves, status-supportive measures to protect or enhance the judges' rank, honors, and tax exemptions).

There were many apparent similarities between court reform in the sixteenth and eighteenth centuries. Very early, one finds expressed the belief, derived from Roman law, that an honest and efficient administration of justice was essential to the prosperity and security of the state and its people. The chapters that follow will show how the concept of reform changed from the sixteenth to the eighteenth century, how reforms were put into practice, and how beliefs about court reform were carried into the early years of the Revolution.

# 1 / Judicial Reform in the Sixteenth and Seventeenth Centuries

The kings of medieval France set up their law courts early, carefully, and vigorously. For it was by establishing their network of justice that they extended and secured their authority.[1] By the early sixteenth century, the crown seemed to have gained, in this manner, full control of the realm. Machiavelli, who went on several diplomatic missions to France before 1512, noted the thorough reduction of the great lords. The crown had checked their "ambition and insolence" by putting "a bit in their mouths." The "bit" was royal justice, administered chiefly by the parlements. Because of the parlements, France was singularly "well ordered and governed."[2]

The Wars of Religion showed, unhappily, that the lords could all too easily shake loose their bit. The kingdom nearly split apart. As royal officials worked to save the authority of the crown, they logically directed much of their activity toward reforming the courts, but the results of their efforts were meager. Exhaustion and stalemate, not the restraining power of any royal institution, brought an end to the fighting. As Henry IV and his successors restored the crown's authority, they reexamined their medieval forebears' approach of basing that authority on courts of law. The absolutist rule of the Bourbons relied instead on intendants.

The courts served the crown so poorly in the latter part of the sixteenth century because, ironically, of certain characteristics that the crown had allowed to develop. The courts had become the guardians of the constitution of the state; most of the offices in the courts had become venal; and the holders of the offices had risen to high social status. Each of these characteristics may earlier have served an end of state, but each later contributed to the unmaking of the state. I shall begin by examining these characteristics, how they evolved and what problems they occasioned, and then discuss programs for reform, where they succeeded and when they fell short.

*Justice at the Service of Ends of State*

"This monarchy more than any other," Machiavelli said of France, "is governed by laws and ordinances." This was so because of the parlements, which guarded the laws "by executions against some of the princes of the realm, and at times even by decisions against the king himself."[3] Claude de Seyssel also observed how the parlements served as a *frein* ("restraint") on the French crown. In his *Monarchie de France* of 1515, he affirmed the importance of the parlements in terms much like Machiavelli's. "Justice," he said, "is more empowered [*autorisée*] in France than in any other country in the world that one knows of . . . because of the parlements, which have been instituted principally for that advocacy and to the end of restraining the absolute power that the kings would like to exercise."[4]

For the custom was that the king asked the parlements to register each new law of his. Before they complied with his request, the parlements, as the custom had further developed, considered the law and determined whether or not it was consistent with the "fundamental laws," or constitution, of the realm. If they felt that it was not, they remonstrated with the king and sometimes got him to modify or even withdraw it. In the Ordonnance of Moulins in 1566, the crown formally recognized the judges' right of remonstration, while placing some limitations on it.[5]

Much symbolic importance attached to the registration of laws. Philippe de Commynes noted that treaties not recorded in the Parlement of Paris were held to be invalid, and he told of Louis XI's anxiousness to register there a treaty that he had concluded with the duke of Burgundy.[6] Whether the importance of registration had originally been promoted by the king or maintained against the king by the parlementaires is unclear. François Hotman was convinced of the former, but he said, in his *Francogallia* of 1573, that the crown had meant to enlarge rather than limit its power by having the parlements register its laws. In Hotman's view, the crown had created the parlements not only to administer justice but also to take over from the council the role of deliberating on new laws. The crown had meant to transfer the "power, dominion, and authority" of the council to a smaller, more "accommodating" group. By this bold stroke, however, the crown only whipsawed itself. For the parlementaires turned out to be wilier than the councillors. "Such was the craft of these men over the last three hundred years or so," said Hotman of the parlementaires, "that not only have they now virtually crushed the authority of the public council . . . , but also they have obliged all the princes of the kingdom, and even the royal majesty itself, to yield to their might."[7]

Another view has seen the parlements achieving their constitutional position with no intentional assistance from the crown. According to Guy Coquille, the sovereign courts were established "for the cases of individuals [*causes des particuliers*] and not for affairs of state."[8] In the version of Voltaire, the kings had had the parlements enregister their laws only "to have a sure deposit in the hands of a permanent and peaceable company," the kings having previously lost their cartularies in wars.[9] As the parlementaires had gained a separate corporate identity and interests occasionally different from those of the crown, however, they had naturally taken advantage of their function of enregistering the laws.

However the parlements had arrived at their position in the state, their guardianship of the constitution began to trouble the crown exceedingly. During the religious wars, parlementaires took stands as extreme as anyone else's and at several times actually opposed the crown. "It is a bad example and confusion in justice," L'Hospital rebuked the Parlement of Paris in 1563, "[for you] to respect some ordonnances and not others . . . At present one has ceased the clamor against the Church, and one cries out against justice. Think, that the judges, in part, are cause of civil wars; *quia addicere animos audacibus et improbis.*"[10] The parlements vexed royal ministers during the seventeenth century as well. Michel de Marillac, frustrated by the Parlement of Paris in his attempts at state reform, wrote a "Mémoire dressé principalement contre l'autorité du Parlement."[11] Anne of Austria and Cardinal Mazarin found their rule challenged during the Fronde of the Parlement.

While the role of the parlements developed with respect to the constitution, offices in the parlements became venal. Judges in the seventeenth and eighteenth centuries defended their property in offices by arguing that it gave them independence, that it allowed them to remonstrate with the king without fear of losing their judgeships.[12] The *inamovibilité* ("irremovability") that the judges believed was insured solely by the ownership of their offices, had, however, actually been legislated by Louis XI.[13] If anything, the guarantee of inamovibilité had opened the way for the sale of offices. As Charles Loyseau pointed out in his *Les cinq livres du droit des offices* (1610), the guarantee that they would not be removed from their offices at the whim of the king was precisely the assurance that people needed before they would lay down their money for the offices. "It is easy to understand," he said, "why we have not practiced this public sale of offices for a long time, inasmuch as the officers were always dismissible [*destituable*], just as simple *commissions* are at present, and were made perpetual only by the Ordonnance of Louis XI of the year 1467, so that there was scarcely any appearance before that time that anyone wanted to purchase these offices."[14]

The higher judicial offices apparently became venal only during the reigns of Louis XII and François I. Few parlements, however, were as bold and innovative in their remonstrances as those of Charles VII,[15] while the parlements of Louis XIV were as ineffective as those of Louis XI in restraining the royal will. The importance of the right to remonstrate varied from reign to reign.

If the venality of judicial offices did not matter for the constitutional role of the parlements, it did affect the administration of justice. Judicial offices were needlessly multiplied so that more would be available for sale. The useless officers thus created, since they were inadequately paid by the crown, supported themselves at the expense of litigants. Trials were prolonged and appeals were encouraged, it was said, long past the point where legal costs exceeded the amount at issue so that judges could collect more épices and lawyers more fees. One of the litigants in Racine's *Les plaideurs* (1669) relates that he has spent fifteen or twenty years—his vagueness on this point reveals in itself how numbing such protracted litigation must have been—and "around" five to six thousand francs in legal actions to recover damages for two bales of hay that his neighbor's foal had eaten on his estate.[16] But already in the second half of the sixteenth century a writer stated that Frenchmen "consume themselves and destroy each other, without much occasion . . . It is nearly impossible to render justice . . . There are more litigants in our realm than in all the rest of Europe."[17] And Jean Bodin wrote, "Frenchmen are so sharpwitted in raising suits as that there is no point of the law, no sillable, no letter, out of which they cannot wrest either true or at least wise probable arguments and reasons."[18]

While some cases were perpetuated, others were said to be ignored. Judges who had invested large sums in their offices, desiring a return on their investments, concentrated, it was thought, on the cases producing the most fees and neglected criminal cases and the small civil suits of those who could not afford to pay what Racine's litigant could. The "avarice" of the judges, said Jean Domat, had led to

> the cessation of the functions of justice in two sorts of situations where the judges cannot excuse themselves from it: in public crimes when there is no other party than the public and in the cases of the poor who demand justice but are incapable, due to their poverty, of paying for the work of the judge. We put in the same category the public interest without party and that of the poor because the one and the other are equally important and commanded, and equally abandoned and neglected.[19]

The failure of the courts to deal with criminal cases was all the more serious because of the amount of crime in the sixteenth and seventeenth centuries. One reads in the second Ordonnance of Blois (May 1579) of persons who made a profession "of killing, committing outrages, overstepping any bounds, and helping prisoners for crimes to escape from the hands of justice—all for money or other compensation."[20] Banditry and brigandage were rife throughout the Mediterranean world in those centuries, Fernand Braudel has said, reaching a great intensity around 1650. Crime surged, according to Braudel, because of greater poverty, created and reinforced by an accentuation of class differences. The growth of town life and the breakup of the traditional manorial community caused general social unrest. Many people were set adrift, and some took to lawlessness, partaking in a flourishing criminal subculture.[21] Also, increasing commerce and especially the conversion to a money economy made robbery more practical and profitable. Coins, which are portable, transferable, and readily negotiable, are easier to steal than livestock.

Small civil suits demanding attention were also plentiful in the sixteenth and seventeenth centuries, precisely when the established courts were said to be inclined not to deal with them. Again, the growth in commercial activity would have been partly responsible: with more trading contacts must have come many disputes of all magnitudes. The uncertainty in the terms of feudal and manorial landholding and tenancy agreements resulting from the transition

LE SEPTRE DE MILICE.

L. Gaultier fecit.

Apres l'honneur des Martiaux Combats    Garder les bons et punir les Cautelles
Faire Iustice et trancher les Debats    Des Plaideureaux Sont vertus immortelles.

1. *Le septre de milice* (*Henry IV*), by Léonard Gaultier. From Ange Cappel, *L'advis donne au roy sur l'abréviation des procès* (Paris? ca. 1600).

that Marc Bloch described to notions of property more influenced by Roman law must surely have led to its share of court cases as well.[22]

As it saw litigation multiply while many deserving cases went unheard, and as it saw crime go unchecked, the public looked to the crown for relief. The crown, in turn, tried to discipline its courts and repair the ill effects of the judges' ownership of their offices. As long, however, as their offices did represent an investment to them, the judges could be expected to use the courts to make money for themselves. People saw that getting them to act otherwise would be extremely difficult. "Each officer," said Coquille, "who has emptied so much money from his household in purchasing his office has wanted not only to replace it but also to make himself rich, that which cannot be without vexation of the people."[23]

In the last of his five books, Rabelais wrote a scathing satire of the judges on account of their avaricious collection of épices. Clawpuss and the Furrycats carry as their "badge and symbol an open pouch," and "plunder is their motto."[24] Justice was traditionally portrayed as a vigilant maiden with the scales of justice in her left hand, balanced, and the sword of retribution in her right. "Justice is represented very properly," said L'Hospital, "by Orpheus, by Hesiod and other ancient poets, in the form of a chaste and modest virgin, come from the sky, and daughter of Jupiter."[25] Michel Colombe sculpted a demure Anne of Brittany as "Justice" for the tomb of the dukes of Brittany in the Cathedral of Nantes (see the frontispiece). In the court of Clawpuss, however, Justice was an old hag who held "a sickle-case in her right hand, and a scales in her left ... The dishes of the scales were a couple of velvet pouches, one full of bullion and hanging down, the other empty and suspended high above the beam."[26]

Incredible as it may seem, the crown apparently had no motive for putting judicial, or, for that matter, any other, offices up for sale except its pressing need for money. There had been for the king, said Richelieu, "no better and quicker expedient for getting voluntarily the property of his subjects than that of giving them honor for money."[27] The sale of offices may have been practiced occasionally during the Middle Ages. It was significant, however, only from around 1500. Louis XII was widely accused of taking money for offices; François I created offices expressly for selling, and he set up the

Bureau des Parties Casuelles in 1522 to receive the income from their sale. Henry II was even more open than his father and abandoned the fiction that the purchasers of offices were only making a "loan" to the crown. In 1598 the oath that new judges had previously been required to take, that they had not paid any money for their offices, was abolished, although as early as 1575 new officers in the Parlement of Paris had been permitted to dispense with the oath by letters patent.[28] By the latter part of the sixteenth century, thousands of offices on all levels, financial as well as judicial, had been sold. The crown had created an "ungovernable number of officers, which is so very great that it is almost easier to chance upon an officer than to find a man without office."[29]

So shocking and enormous and unfortunate an innovation did contemporaries believe the sale of offices to be that they could not accept its being to any extent indigenous. Rather, said Coquille, the French had learned about selling offices during their wars in Italy. The kings had been "badly counseled," he said, by those who had "insinuated themselves into the favors and good graces of the kings as flatterers are wont to do," to follow the Italian practice of selling offices to get money. For the venality of offices was, in his view, one of the causes of the miseries of France; it had led to the "contemnement de Justice," which in turn had led people to seek their own, extrajudicial remedies.[30]

Bodin excoriated the sale of judicial offices in particular as a sacrilege and for its destructive consequences. It was to him "the most dangerous and pernitious plague in a Commonweale ... They which make sale of estates, offices, and benefices, they sell the most sacred thing in the world which is Justice, they sell the Commonweale, they sell the bloud of the subjects, they sell the lawes, and taking away all the rewards of honor, vertue, learning, pietie, and religion, they open the gates to thefts, corruption, covetousness, injustice, arrogancie, impietie, and to be short, to all vice and villainie."[31] Bodin cited the ascent of L'Hospital, "a poore Physitians sonne [become] Chauncellour of a great kingdome," as a stellar example of the proper working of a commonwealth: "for [his] noble vertues were worthily exalted even unto the highest degrees of honours."[32] Yet the chancellor said that the necessity of buying offices was increasingly preventing the ablest, who, as a consequence of their long studies, were sometimes also among the poorest, from obtaining positions, "knowledge and virtue without money being counted for nothing."[33] La Popelinière, the Protestant historian, also decried the way in which the sale of offices allowed people "vilely to acquire by money that which they should obtain by virtue," saying that the king should freely elect—that is, without being influenced by money—those who "feared God."[34] For the sale of offices deprived the kings of the control over the administration of justice believed to be essential to sound government and the peace and security of the realm. The venality of offices was also seen as wrong in itself; justice would not be reformed without its abolition.

The sale of offices was further deplored for retarding the political economy of France. At first, and through the early 1570s, the prices of offices appear to have been set in terms of the king's needs for money rather than in relation to the market value of the offices themselves. During the last quarter of the sixteenth century, however, a "systematic market economy" of offices grew up.[35] From the late sixteenth century through the reign of Louis XIV, the demand for offices was great, and their prices rose almost steadily. Money, more and more of it, that might have been invested in commerce went instead, writers alleged, toward the purchase of offices; talent was diverted from entrepreneurial pursuits. "An infinity of persons," wrote Coquille, "have taken themselves from trade, from the sciences, from the arts, and from financial transactions, which are the true supports of a republic, and have become lazy pot-bellies."[36]

The reason for this abandonment of useful undertakings was thought to be obvious. "No source of gain and return," said L'Hospital, "is more certain today than that of offices. They are not subject to frost or drought; one has never to fear shipwreck, encounters with pirates or brigands; their holders will never face bankruptcy nor any other peril, accident, or natural disaster. The harvest from offices is easy, infallible, and never disappoints the hope of their owners."[37] An office was, in other words, a superior investment, in terms of its appreciation and yield and its security.[38] By the eighteenth century, the prices of offices were falling, and posts in the judiciary may have remained, at best, moderately attractive generators of income.[39] But in the sixteenth century the attractions of offices were manifold.

If officeholders were content, however, the crown had reasons to be miserable. For it had saddled itself with administrators who were not only incorrigible but also expensive. By allowing money that might otherwise have been invested in industry and commerce to be put into offices, the crown sacrificed national production and hence slowed the growth of its ordinary revenues. More immediately, the crown had to pay out annually the gages on each officer's investment. While it spent right away what it got from selling an office, the crown owed the gages on the office forever. By the middle of the seventeenth century, the crown apparently owed, if it did not always pay, much more in gages each year than it took in from selling offices and collecting the various premiums, such as the *droit annuel* and *suppléments de finances,* that it extracted from those who already had offices.[40] That Louis XIV continued and even enlarged the sale of offices was only another example of that king's shortsighted pursuit of immediate gain at the long-run expense of the kings who would come after him.

Initially a source of income, then, the sale of offices became, in short order, the source of a considerable drain on royal resources as well as the cause of gross inefficiencies and injustices. As financial expedients go, it was a particularly maladroit one.

The third new characteristic of the French judiciary in the early modern period—the high social status of its members—also had an effect that the crown had not envisioned. The crown accorded "honors, prerogatives, and distinctions" to its officeholders, giving the officeholders a social rank as well as a public function.[41] The crown intended to insure the loyalty of its officers by so distinguishing them and also to give the officers the social confidence they would need to confront the nobility. In a society of only three estates, however, the king's raising the judges to the top of the Third Estate only whetted their appetites and made them push to be included in the Second Estate, among the nobility. Dependent on the crown for their privileges, the judges naturally sought the clear title to their privileges that noble status alone seemed to signify. Even before the king began to give in and make offices in the parlements ennobling, judges identified with noble causes, sometimes uniting with the nobility against the crown.

The judicial bourgeoisie that grew up in France was thus differentiated from the rest of the bourgeoisie by status, aspirations, and attitudes as well as by profession. Its emergence within the Third Estate disrupted the neat division of French society into three estates. Its development into a *noblesse de robe* ("judicial nobility") necessitated a reconceptualization of society that was never accomplished. The social and political uncertainties caused by the rise of the judges had their analogue in theoretical confusion. As did the constitutional assertions of the parlements and the parlementaires' ownership of office, the social dynamism of the judges prompted endless speculation about the history, nature, purpose, and hierarchy of Old Regime institutions. Intended by the crown to stabilize and quiet the kingdom, the judges instead made it turbulent. Adding epicycles to the theory of monarchy and traditional society to account for the movements of the courts and their members did no good. In the end it only overburdened the theory, which, like the Aristotelian-Ptolemaic theory of the universe, finally collapsed under the prodigious weight of its accumulated contradictions, taking with it in the eighteenth century the unaccountable regime that it purported to explain. More than any other institution, the judiciary, not least by disconcerting people and causing them to reexamine their society in order to accommodate it, was responsible for the undoing of the Old Regime.

### Efforts to Reform an Intractable Judiciary

Conventional wisdom in sixteenth- and seventeenth-century France frowned on reform. The Wars of Religion, emerging as they did from the Reformation and the Counter Reformation, left Frenchmen skeptical of the motives not only of religious but of all other reformers and doubtful that any of their programs would help the kingdom. "As for externals," said Montaigne, "[the wise man] should wholly follow the accepted fashions and forms." "For whoever meddles," he continued, "with choosing and changing usurps the authority to judge, and he must be very sure that he sees the weakness of what he is casting out and the goodness of what he is bringing in."[42] A century later, La Bruyère remarked, "There are certain ills in the State which are endured because they avert or prevent greater ills. There are others which are evil only because of the way they have become established, and which, springing originally from some abuse or undesirable custom, are less harmful in their consequences and in practice than a juster law or a more rational tradition."[43] It was the same posture that Descartes had taken in warning his readers not to undertake or even to contemplate reform of the state.

L'Hospital, Bodin, and Richelieu took a similar attitude because of their experience and the moderate precepts of their classical education. "It is necessary, truly," said L'Hospital, "to accommodate oneself to the ways of the times in which we live, and one will gain nothing from blindfolding oneself against the laws and the rigor of necessity."[44] "That it is a most dangerous thing," stated Bodin, "at one and the selfe same time, to chaunge the forme, lawes, and customes of a Commonweale."[45] "At the new establishment of a republic," explained Richelieu, "one would be shamed not to banish venality, because reason demands that one establish the most perfect laws that the society of men can bear. But prudence does not allow acting in the same way in an old monarchy, in which the imperfections have passed into custom and in which disorder makes, not without utility, part of the order of the state."[46]

The practical results of this cautious or distrustful view of reform were that little was changed and nothing was abolished. At most, the leaders of the old institutions were reprimanded or new institutions to fill the roles that the old ones had neglected were set up alongside of them. Hence were created, in the sixteenth century, the prévôts des maréchaux, the présidiaux, and the tribunaux consulaires, among others, and, in the early seventeenth, the intendants. Officials talked, at times, a great deal about reforming the old institutions. During the religious wars, L'Hospital urged the abolition of the venality of judicial offices, going so far, perhaps, as proposing how it could be accomplished and the restoration of a "virtuous" judiciary achieved.[47] He appears, though, never seriously to have attempted this structural reform, and he stayed for the most part with organizational and disciplinary measures. By the time of Richelieu, the cardinal's statement suggests, the kings and their ministers saw their options as so limited and were so temperamentally averse to reform that they had stopped considering significant changes in the institutions they had inherited. It was perhaps also due in part to the depth and persistence of the French skepticism of reform that the Fronde was so much less serious and concerted than the revolution of the English Puritans.

Insofar as it was considered, change, through the sixteenth and into the seventeenth century, meant traditional reform. All the court reforms proposed or enacted were "to shape again or remold, to alter or amend, to restore or reestablish" the judiciary. The shortcomings in the administration of justice were thought to result either from the courts' having departed from what they had been originally, in medieval times, or from their not having been modeled closely enough after the courts of ancient times. The law courts of the reign of Louis IX were especially admired. Then French justice had been so esteemed that other countries had sent cases to be adjudicated in France. When people spoke of reducing the judiciary to manageable size, they had in mind returning to the number of court officers in the golden age of Louis XII ("the father of the people"), or at least the earlier part of that king's reign, before the sale of offices had begun to swell the judiciary out of all proportion. (Later, when hopes of going back to the golden ages of Louis IX and Louis XII had dimmed, the âge d'or was moved ahead. Some of those in the eighteenth century who still envisioned such an age held that it existed during the reign of Henry IV.)

And in one of the commonest, and perhaps most simple-minded, proposals for reducing the burgeoning number of civil suits, Ange Cappel recommended that the losers of court cases be fined. After all, he stated, the Egyptians had levied such fines, and the practice was later observed by the Hebrews ("as stated by the rabbi Maynon [Maimonides?] in his treatise on Hebrew law and order"), passed on to the Athenian Greeks, borrowed by the Romans, confirmed and renewed by the emperor Justinian, and used by the Italians and the French.[48] (Others who proposed fining those defeated in court included Philibert Bonet, who urged the mulcting of both the losing litigants and the lawyers who had assisted them and "by their temerities made their clients ruin and consume themselves";[49] François Du Noyer, who wanted "all parties who succumb . . . be it in the first instance or on appeal" to be amerced;[50] and, as late as the eighteenth century, Diderot.)[51]

The traditional nature of early reform may also be seen in attempts during the sixteenth and seventeenth centuries to alter or remedy the ill effects of the three unruly characteristics of the judiciary described above. The constitutional role of the parlements, first of all, provoked the crown on several occasions to limit the right of remonstrance. The most noteworthy of these was in 1673, when Louis XIV decreed that the parlements could exercise their right of remonstrance only after they had registered the laws that he had sent them.

In so decreeing, Louis XIV was following the course set by his father in 1641 with his more qualified limitation of parlementary remonstrations. Indeed, one of the issues of the Fronde had been the apparent policy of the crown to circumscribe the parlements. A pamphlet of 1652 accused the crown of wanting to confine the parlements to the causes des particuliers—which it had not succeeded in doing when it established them—so that it could violate the laws as it chose.[52] In actuality, however, the crown at no time curbed the parlements in so drastic a way as Maupeou did. Nor did it consider the kind of radical reform comprised by Lamoignon's experiment on the eve of the Revolution with the cours plenières, in which the crown sought a wholly new way of getting its laws recorded. Disciplining the parlements was one thing; purging or seeking an alternative to them was, or should have been, quite another. By doing the former, the crown returned the parlements to the bounds that it deemed appropriate to them; by succeeding at the latter, the crown would have created a new order for the state.

Efforts to come to grips with the problems created by the sale of judicial offices were more complex, but once again their traditional pattern was set. The prévôts des maréchaux, présidiaux, and tribunaux consulaires, all of which were set up to expedite the justice that the sale of offices had indirectly slowed, were linked to the past. François I created the prévôts des maréchaux, or judges of the military police, to pass sentence "in the first instance and without appeal" in cases such as housebreaking, highway robbery, sedition, and riot.[53] He stamped these judges with the fearsome likeness of the summary justice of Anglo-Saxon and Germanic law and of Roman military jurisdictions. Part of a general repression of criminality, the prévots des maréchaux were of a piece with the harsh procedural and other enactments of the Ordonnance of Villers-Cotterêts (1539), authored by Chancellor Guillaume Poyet, and the introduction of crueler modes of punishment, including the wheel, which is said to have been brought to France from Germany by Poyet's predecessor, Antoine du Bourg.[54]

The présidiaux, created by edict of Henry II in 1551–1552, were designed to fill the function not being served adequately by the bailliages and sénéchaussées of limiting the number of cases going

2. *La couronne de justice* (*Marie de Médicis*), by Thomas de Leu. From Ange Cappel, *L'advis donne au roy sur l'abréviation des procès* (Paris? ca. 1600).

to the parlements. Contemporaries accused the impecunious king of creating the présidial offices mainly so that he could sell them. Many local cahiers drawn up for Estates-General from the second half of the sixteenth century through 1614 called for their suppression.[55] Nevertheless, the erection of the présidiaux was consistent with the reforms preceding it and when viewed alongside of them may be seen as yet another move to speed up justice—here, civil as well as criminal—in times of alarming disorder. Hence when the crown stated in the preamble to the edict of creation that its intent was to streamline appeals, it was quite probably telling at least part of the truth.

The présidiaux were superimposed, initially, on sixty or so of the bailliages and sénéchaussées—as the lower courts were called variously depending on where in France they were—and given final jurisdiction over civil suits valued up to a certain amount and over some criminal cases. The présidiaux were meant to ease the crowded dockets of the parlements and to allow litigants and criminal defendants to get final justice closer to their homes and thus at less expense and inconvenience to themselves.[56] From the very start, however, the parlements resisted the intrusion on their sources of income that the présidiaux represented—the parlements prospered from their crowded dockets—and did everything that they could to thwart the présidiaux in the exercise of their jurisdictions. Litigants, for their part, often aided the parlements in this sabotage by choosing the higher justice of the parlements, whenever they could obtain it, over the justice of the présidiaux.

The most damaging *coups de bec,* though, were delivered by the steady reduction, due to inflation, of the real value of the monetary limit on the size of civil suits over which the présidiaux had final cognizance. As the crown, due largely to pressure from the parlements, failed to raise the limit, the number of cases coming before the présidiaux diminished. By the eighteenth century, the présidiaux were moribund. Many of their offices could find no purchasers. The présidiaux tried to recoup their loss of cases to the parlements by asserting their right of *prévention* ("claim of prior jurisdiction") over cases in the seignorial courts, but that tended to make a bad impression, without compensating for the value of the cases that the présidiaux were losing. Coquille, for one, urged that seignorial courts be defended against incursions by the présidiaux—

and also by the prévôts des maréchaux—by limiting préventions. Realistically, he also urged that the parlements be forbidden from contravening the jurisdictions of the présidiaux and prévôts so that these new courts would not find it necessary to go after the cases in the seignorial courts.[57]

Despite their mediocre record, the présidiaux stayed in jurists' minds, where they appeared in the eighteenth century as models for reformed courts. Continual attempts were made during that century to revive the présidiaux or to create other courts like them. The reason for this later interest in the présidiaux was that these jurisdictions, while traditional in conception, had what could be seen as a proto-modern aspect. Namely, their *ressorts* ("jurisdictions") were established according to canons of convenience and need, regardless of and even cutting across the historic, territorial divisions that had formerly determined where courts were to be situated. "The présidial seats," said Coquille, "have not any mark of province, region, and territory and were established in recent memory, forty years ago, to judge small cases without appeal; and in establishing them one had not regard to the distinction of provinces but solely to the proximity [of the présidiaux to the justiciables], in order to render Justice more easily."[58] In the sixteenth century the ressorts of the présidiaux were seen to follow simply from the medieval principle of bringing justice closer to the people—although even then such ressorts may have been somewhat alien to many, which could account in part for the courts' lack of acceptance. But in the eighteenth century these ressorts could be regarded as an early example of how the country might be redivided into "rational" judicial—and also administrative—units.

The tribunaux consulaires, patterned after medieval modes of arbitration and judgment by one's peers, were another new jurisdiction set up in the sixteenth century to expedite justice. Original jurisdiction over disputes between *négociants* ("great wholesale merchants"), *marchands* ("small to medium sized wholesalers or retailers"), and *navigateurs* ("sea merchants") was separated from the ordinary courts and reassigned to these strictly commercial courts. The first of them was created at Toulouse in 1549. L'Hospital's establishment of one in Paris in 1563 marked official recognition of the quickening pace and increasing complexity of commerce. Many disputes between merchants were arising; the merchants wanted quick adjudication of them so that they could proceed with their affairs; and the ordinary courts, preoccupied as they were with lengthening proceedings to gain more fees, could not be relied upon to act speedily enough. The tribunaux consulaires were staffed by members of the local business communities and were empowered to try commercial cases, in the first instance, "without long proceedings, nor the formality of pleading."[59]

The parlements, of course, fought this further invasion of their jurisdictions, and the new tribunals were not multiplied rapidly enough to handle the volume of commercial cases. Ordinary courts continued to take cognizance over most of the cases.[60] The new tribunals also, despite their composition, perfected their own corrupt practices.[61] But notwithstanding the consular tribunals' flaws and abuses, merchants found them indispensable and pressed for them everywhere. As further testimony to their important function, the commercial courts were one of the few French institutions to survive the Revolution of 1789 virtually intact.

In addition to experimenting with judicial organization, early reformers considered, though only for a time, structural change. The ending of the venality of offices and the institution of free justice (*la justice gratuite*)—the latter, so that no cases would be more attractive to judges financially than any others—were fervently advocated. When the question was raised, though, of how the sale of offices was to be reversed and free justice established, few had an answer. A rearrangement and expansion of royal finances would obviously have been required. For the cost of buying back judicial offices would have been enormous. And in order to have banned the collection of épices, judges' gages would have had to be augmented. For even jurists who urged judges to let virtue be its own reward and to "leave profit to the merchants" acknowledged that the gages the judges received were insufficient.

L'Hospital and, in the early seventeenth century, François Du Noyer put forward two plans for financing a restructured judiciary. While Du Noyer's was especially ambitious, both men's plans were strictly traditional in that they would have attempted structural reform through fiscal ingenuity rather than statutory boldness, a tack that would be tried again, though with some new twists, a hundred years after Du Noyer's work by the duc d'Orléans and John Law.

The crown should put "a well-instructed man," said L'Hospital, in charge of paying out augmented gages to judges from a *fonds* ("estate" or "fund") that would be created and maintained at the expense neither of the "finances of his majesty" nor of "the throngs of his impoverished people." These new gages would be true wages, not interest payments, and they would be apportioned among judges according to the amount of work that each judge did. The superintendent of the gages would be forbidden to pay any gages to lazy, negligent, or absentee judges, under pain of having to make them up out of his own pocket; the amount of gages thus forfeited by judges would be given to "the poor of the Conciergerie." Gages would be raised periodically, "at the good pleasure of the king . . . according to . . . [the judges'] merits."[62]

Apparently from the same fonds, officers, starting with the lowest, auxiliary ones, were to be reimbursed the price of their offices. For not only, in L'Hospital's view, had the crown to stop making and selling offices, it had also to regain control over the officers that it had by gradually buying back their offices so that it could begin discharging the great many that it did not need.[63] As the collection of épices led to the corruption of justice, so the venality of offices led to the cumbersome size of the judiciary. Justice could never be honest and efficient without the abolition of both.[64]

What L'Hospital had in mind by his fonds is obscure. He did not specify, at least in the portion of his work that has survived, the source of the monies or other resources that were to have gone into it. L'Hospital did not intend, though, that augmented gages would ever equal the income that judges derived from épices. A reduction in the judges' income would be made possible by a moral refurbishment of the judicial corps. L'Hospital stated again and again that judges should find greater satisfaction in honor than in remuneration. His lack of detail about the fonds may indicate his beliefs that the first priority of the crown should be restoring the judges' morals and that subsequently the financing, which then would not, perhaps, be so very costly, would somehow take care of itself.

In March 1613, the king's council issued an *arrêt* calling for justice free of charge; delegates to the Estates-General of 1614 evidently talked about how "free justice" could be implemented. In the wake of the Estates, François Du Noyer submitted a proposal to the crown in which he drew, he said, upon some of the ideas that the Estates had discussed.[65] Like L'Hospital, Du Noyer sought both to end the collection of épices and pay the judges adequate gages instead, and to stop the sale of offices ("la ... damnable coustume qui s'est comme un serpent glissée parmy la France") and repurchase offices already sold. But he gave a better idea than L'Hospital how the necessary fonds would be managed and from where it would come.

A "Bureau général" and a "Banque royale" were to be set up in Paris, and a network of branch offices set up in "other cities and parishes of the realm," all under the direction of a board including the king's council, the Compagnie du Commerce, and "Messieurs de la Justice." This "Compagnie de la Justice" would be organized roughly along the lines of the ferme générale and the royal treasury; it would collect money after the fashion of the former and pay out money in the manner of the latter. The company would either be granted or allowed to use certain resources, which it would invest and manage so as to yield a profit. With its profit it would: (1) buy back offices—not only judicial, but financial, governmental, and military as well—when they fell vacant upon the deaths or resignations of their current holders, when all offices would revert to the crown; (2) pay officials wages commensurate with their "rank and quality"; and, after a period, (3) repay the crown, with interest, the value of the resources that the crown had let the company use. The crown would grant the company the right to fines from litigants and others who abused the court system and perpetual control of all goods and other property "seized by authority of Justice" or vacated and abandoned, along with the right to the income from any leases or other obligations pertaining thereto. It would allow the company to manage property held by minors and the mentally incompetent. And it would create *rentes* ("annuities"), loosely speaking, from some of its *droits,* or rights, including those to "godsends [e.g., treasure-troves], escheats, and wrecks" and those of *lods et ventes* and *quints et requints.* The crown would give these droits to the company in return for the company's obliging itself to refund their value, plus interest ("au denier vingt"), five years later.

The crown's revenue would not be diminished, even in the initial period before the company had begun to repay the revenues or droits that the crown had allowed it to divert to its use. For the company was also to police the collection of all of the king's revenues and to supervise "all contracts, writs, bills of exchange, and promissory notes, in order to avoid the abuses that are committed daily."

That new policing, coupled with the phasing out of venal financial officers, would, thought Du Noyer, make the crown's financial machine run much more smoothly and eliminate much fraud from the political economy in general. The economy of the kingdom would thrive and the amount of the ordinary revenues of the crown reaching the crown would escalate. Thus would be reversed the sale of offices and its retarding economic effects.

The shortcomings in Du Noyer's proposal are readily found. He gave no figures or estimates of the money amounts of any of the revenues and expenditures that he discussed. Whether his scheme was practicable or not is thus hard to say. Furthermore, because he was vague as to how the bank would value the "deposits" of its resources and those of its branches, he does not give one confidence that his bank would have controlled the money supply.

If a local office was short of money, Du Noyer stated, the central bank would grant it a mortgage on some of the property that it was allowed to hold under his proposal, "since nothing is easier than paying off mortgages." This would keep the office from having to get the funds that it needed "through the hands of usurers." So as not to put the system "in ruins" by overextending its indebtedness, no office, nor the central bank (which could presumably have borrowed from the local offices), would have been allowed to borrow more than the value of its current non-monetary resources and of the interest or other resources that it expected to receive in the future. But it would have been allowed to borrow that, and that sounds like an indeterminable amount. Whether anyone at the time realized just how much discipline is required of a central banker for a system like Du Noyer's to work is questionable. In some respects, indeed, Du Noyer's bank could have been a prototype of John Law's. Its assets, if not imaginary, as were some of Law's, were problematical and unpredictable.

Others who touched on the subject of the cost of justice usually recommended only that judges be prompted by counsels of moderation in their collection of épices. And, if they deplored the venality of judicial offices, they had, or at least offered, no ideas of how to end it. One Jean Mille, the author of a manual on criminal law in 1541, urged judges not to receive presents, "since presents close the eyes of the wise and alter the word of the just." He eased his injunction, however, by saying that it was all right for judges to collect true épices (things that were edible and that one consumed right away), and that it was also appropriate for judges to accept horses as gifts. Neither food nor horses—so long, that is, as judges did not descend into "cupidity" by taking them in excessive quantities—would, Mille thought, influence judges' decisions.[66] Bodin, too, merely urged judges to be moderate and reasonable in their collection of épices and to assess litigants according to their wealth and ability to pay.[67]

The moral suasions, accompanied by internal regulation of épices by the courts and supervision by the intendants, seem to have done some good. Indictments of judicial immorality like those of the sixteenth century still appeared in the eighteenth century, though judicial prejudice and bigotry were the increasingly frequent targets.[68] But the indictments sound stale, and alongside of them one finds the remarks of a foreign observer, Adam Smith: "Those parliaments are perhaps, in many respects, not very convenient courts of justice; but they have never been accused; they seem never even to have been suspected of corruption."[69] Structural changes would still be desired, however, for reasons that seemed equally compelling.

As for the transformation of the judicial bourgeoisie into a noblesse de robe and its progressive fusion with the *noblesse d'épée* ("military nobility"), the crown, while promoting the former, tried, of course, to check the latter. Through sumptuary legislation and strict enforcement of the rules of *préséance* ("precedence"), the crown attempted to maintain the distinctions and social distance between the two nobilities. Such means were obviously wholly traditional. They were undermined by the purchase of judicial posts by sword nobility,[70] by intermarriage and other social unions, and, due to the dormancy of the Estates-General between 1614 and 1789, by the lack or inadequacy of any prominent institutions other than the parlements to put forward and defend the *thèse nobiliaire* ("aristocratic thesis," as opposed to the *thèse royale*, or "royal thesis" of government).[71]

Like traditional approaches to turning back the development of the constitutional role of the parlements and the sale of offices, early attempts to stop the fusion of robe and sword were hampered by a lack of appreciation for the strength and irreversibility of social and political change. It seems hardly possible that the crown should not have anticipated what would happen once it granted, for instance, perfect nobility to the members of the Parlement of Paris in 1644. It is even harder to grasp how the crown could have thought that regulating the dress, for example, of the officers in its sovereign courts would keep them from identifying with the causes of the sword nobility, with whom they had come to have so much else in common. Still, the crown's efforts here, like its efforts in the other two cases, were not altogether unavailing. The fusion of the two nobilities was never complete, and as late as the Maupeou years the crown was able to profit from rivalry between robe and sword. Before passing judgment on traditional reform, one should remember that modern reform would not be without its shortcomings either.

### The Emergence of Modern Reform

The modern concept of reform took shape gradually. Its influence began to make itself felt distinctly and forcefully in France in the second half of the seventeenth century. It manifested itself in efforts at judicial reform in three ways. Whereas reformers had previously referred to historical precedents to justify the changes that they wished to make, beginning with the reign of Louis XIV reformers contrasted the institutions of their day with ideal institutions, which they had reasoned from principles of justice. And whereas earlier reformers had added jurisdictions or set up additional courts when they saw that the existing ones were not functioning as they had originally been intended to, the modern jurists analyzed the judicial institutions that they had before them and would have radically changed them in order to bring them into conformity with their ideals. Finally, while traditional reformers had seldom expected their efforts to succeed, modern reformers, filled with confidence from their new method and forgetting the problems of putting thought into action, had high hopes of achieving the improvements they sought.

The classical revival of the Renaissance had fostered certain habits of mind, among them that of reasoning by analogy. Indeed, the word *analogique* itself first came into use during the 1540s.[72] In a work originally published in 1579, for instance, Charles de Figon, *maître ordinaire* in the Chambre des comptes at Montpellier, compared the royal administration, with all of its judicial, financial, and other officers, to a tree, "having roots, trunk, boughs, and branches, where one can easily see and recognize . . . the connection and correspondence that they all have to a common stock . . . The fruit that one awaits from this noble plant proceeds from the purity and perfection of its roots, which represent the Conseil d'état and the undertakings of the king."[73] As a tree must be pruned periodically to remove branches that have become "useless or superfluous, damaged and rotted," so had, in the mind of Figon, the "entire regime and government of France" in order to insure the "true and perfect cultivation of this plant."[74]

Analogical reasoning restricted jurists in their choice of models for reform to what existed or had existed. While organic comparisons like Figon's were common, the most frequent analogies were to alleged historical precedents. L'Hospital, for example, argued against the venality of offices in France by showing that under the emperor Caligula, making available "charges et dignités politiques" to those who merely had the most money had had the worst consequences: injustice, atheism, and a bestial and tyrannical government.[75] L'Hospital's work is indeed so peppered with analogies to ancient times that it reads, in places, more like a history of Rome than a treatise on France.

Increasingly, during the sixteenth century, French writers sought precedents for their recommendations in the history of their own country. Etienne Pasquier, in urging that French customary rather than Roman law be the starting point for codification, asserted that the French were clearer minded than the Italians, that French customary law was Christian while Roman law, inappropriately, was pagan, and that the historical development of France was different than that of ancient Rome and thus demanded different legal remedies.[76] (François Hotman, too—in his *Antitribonian*—held that Roman law was "irrelevant" to the French situation;[77] and Bodin feared that subjects' respect for Roman or any other of the "laws of straungers" might detract from their willingness to obey the laws of their own king.)[78] But the basic approach of arguing from past example remained.

The example of Roman law was particularly important to French jurists during the early modern period. Before some of them began to dismiss it as inapplicable to France, they used Roman law as a gauge of the correctness of their own laws and institutions. In brief, Roman law, as embodied in the Code of Justinian (the retrieval of

which, begun in the eleventh and twelfth centuries, culminated in
the sixteenth in France with the works of Jacques Cujas), distinguished between public and private law and provided a ready clas-
sification scheme for laws under each heading. It outlined constitutional arrangements whereby the authority of the ruler was
sovereign ("Princeps legibus solutus est"). And it gave a model of
uniform jurisdictions and the consistent application of a single law
throughout a judicial *system.* To this extent, Roman law prepared
the way for the modern reforms that jurists would later propose.

It was perhaps quite a distance from L'Hospital's rudimentary
formulation of vicious judges causing disorder and misery in the
state to the Physiocrats' relatively sophisticated notions of the function of an efficient judiciary in the political economy. But Roman
law, by stressing the subservience of the judiciary to the legislative
authority and the dependence of order in the state on consistency in
the laws and their application, led jurists to view the state comprehensively and see the role of each of its components, one of them
being the judiciary, in the life of the state.

Philibert Bonet, in his 1556 work on the "means to shorten trials
and remove the impediments to the good and brief expedition of
justice," proposed that the French adopt the stricture from Roman
civil law, *Ne liceat tertio provocare* ("It is not allowed to appeal for the
third time"). Two appeals, he felt, were sufficient to reach a just set-
tlement of any dispute, and ending superfluous appeals was vital for
"providing against slownesses and delays in having justice."[79] The
hierarchy of French courts, like that of ancient Roman courts, was,
in the opinion of Bonet, to be clearly established so that there would
be no doubt in the minds of litigants as to where they might take
their cases on appeal.

In the dedication of his work to Anne, duc de Montmorency,
Bonet stated that despite their having promulgated many good laws
and ordonnances, the French kings had not attained their objective
of making justice "better and more briefly administered":

Great affliction and ruin in the republic proceeded as much from the calumnies
and temerities of litigants, *avocats,* and *procureurs* as from the wrongs of judges. I
was urged . . . by . . . some judges and lawyers who love the good and brief expedition of justice, as well as by the obligation that a subject should feel to be, with
all his strength, of service to the king and to the utility of his republic, to find and
put in writing the means for removing the said impediments to the good and
brief expedition of justice.

As the emperor Justinian had recognized the importance of justice in the state to such a degree that he had set in motion his great commissions, so the French kings, Bonet suggested, should devote a large amount of their attention to it. Bonet quoted from Justinian's prologue to the Institutes, where the emperor had said that the strengths of a king are his might and his justice, and that of the two the greater is his justice. For where justice obtains, the foundation of order is surer. With the order created by efficient justice, said Bonet, come the "prosperity and happiness" of the realm.[80]

In the medieval view, kings were bound, as God's lieutenants on earth, to see that justice was done and that, like God's, it was done surely and swiftly. This was, the kings thought, their primary responsibility as rulers. Justice was manifestly important to social peace and stability and to the political economy, and all kings must surely have recognized the necessity of maintaining the social and economic supports of their rule. But the purely devotional impulse in royal judicial reform predominated during the Middle Ages. During the Renaissance, too, Frenchmen emphasized the divine authority with which the kings had been entrusted. "[Justice]," said Seyssel, "is the first and the most dignified treasure of this realm (after religion . . .), by which, more than by all others, the realm is made illustrious, honored, conserved, and augmented. And by so much is the prince and monarch obliged to maintain and watch over it that he is elected and deputed by divine Providence to this office, so great and so honorable, principally to preserve and administer justice, which is the true function of princes."[81] Later in the century, another jurist noted that the king's judges shared the divine responsibility: "Thus is it the kings and princes who are the ministers and lieutenants of God on earth: who have their eyes that are attentive to their peoples, visit their subjects, defend them from oppression, and administer justice to them. Here is the eye of the king, that is, here are the officers of the king, to execute justice according to his laws, his edicts and ordonnances."[82] L'Hospital's rage over the sale of offices was so great because the chancellor saw justice as "a sacred object, not at all for commerce among men."[83]

To Bonet, justice was still the central attribute of the king, but in addition to being a hallowed end, it was a practical means. Its administration depended not only on the king's virtue and piety, but also on his foresight and ingenuity. It sprang, properly, not only from the imitation of God but also from the needs of the kingdom. In Bonet's exhorting of Henry II to the "great, useful, and necessary work" of reforming justice, one sees the balance shifting, under the weight of the Roman example, toward a functional appreciation of justice. Inspired by the modern idea of reform, later jurists would seek systematically to determine the "utility" of laws.

Most decisive to the course of jurisprudence, however, and most important in the shift from traditional to modern reform was the inspiration that classicism, filtered through and elaborated upon by medieval scholars and theologians, gave jurists to reflect on natural law. Even while jurists of Renaissance France were maintaining that the restoration of the simple, certain, and honest justice of the Middle Ages was more apropos to the problems of justice in their day than the forms of Roman law, this other legal conception of the ancients was drawing them away from their own history once again. Bonet, for instance, justified the measures that he proposed for the reform of French justice not only by showing that they were stipulated in the jus civile. He also asserted that the jus civile was founded in "natural law," in "reason and natural equity," and thus was applicable to France.[84] Finally, toward the end of the seventeenth century, under the additional impetus of their reading of Descartes, some jurists broke loose from the moorings of the past altogether and sought to reconstruct French laws and institutions completely, on natural, universal, and rational grounds. They justified the changes that they urged by showing that they followed logically from the moral principles that they believed "are not enjoined on men by written laws but are observed by unwritten custom and universal practice."[85]

A French jurist in the second half of the seventeenth century who tried fully to integrate natural law with secular justice was Jean Domat. Jurists before Domat's time had often expressed the wish that positive and natural law were one and the same. But they had usually resigned themselves to an inevitable difference between the two. Some had even maintained that one's adherence to natural law could be reasonable and legitimate grounds for revolt or disobedience when the positive law was contrary to it. Domat would not have had such a distinction between positive and natural law. For what earlier jurists had wished, he actively and systematically

worked. In his work, and in that of others like him, was the foundation of the new state that would emerge during the Revolution,
which would peremptorily demand both political and moral subservience from its citizens.

"The duty of judges and the duty of individuals," Domat stated,
"are equally called in the Scripture by the name of justice, because
the justice of men is nothing other than the conformity of their actions to the divine rules of equity."[86] Jurists after Bonet had apparently concluded that neither the jus civile nor the jus gentium
expressed natural law. Their rejection of Roman in favor of medieval French law was probably due in part to their discovery that the
"regularity" of the Code of Justinian, which had in fact been hastily
compiled and was full of contradictions, had been more in the minds
of Renaissance jurists than in the code itself.[87] Domat's self-ap-
pointed mission, therefore—since he still preferred Roman law—
was to reorder the Roman law after the "natural order." Not only
would it then be better, it would also be more easily comprehended
and so possibly more readily adopted by the French.

To explore further the expectations that jurists had of secular justice before Domat, one may examine some of the definitions that the
jurists gave to *justice*. Seyssel, first of all, in the early sixteenth century, viewed the justice of men almost exclusively as an institution,
which was to insure "harmony and decorum" among the three estates. Seeing, like Machiavelli, that the principal threat of disorder
came from the nobility—"which has the arms"—Seyssel looked to
the courts to "prevent and punish" any "outrages" that the Second
Estate might attempt or commit against the other two. Justice,
again as an institution, also restrained the king from acting tyranni-
cally.[88] To Seyssel, secular justice, the justice of the courts, would
clearly be doing well to apply the positive laws and protect the fundamental laws of the kingdom.

Writing about a half century later, L'Hospital also looked to justice to maintain the tranquility and order of the state.[89] But though
he had perhaps far less reason to than Seyssel, he went on to state
that he could not be satisfied with justice that did only that. He defined a principle by which secular justice should guide itself. "The
definition of justice," he said, "is a constant and perpetual will to
protect and offer to each person what is his, what belongs to him,

even in this corrupt time that, to be brought to rectitude, must be
bent to the opposite, like the bow or the bent rod."[90] When a kingdom is without that kind of justice, stated L'Hospital, quoting Saint
Augustine, it ceases to be a kingdom. It is then no more than "a true
brigandage," "a true cut-throat locality."[91] (The influence of Saint
Augustine, indeed—through its presence in both Protestantism and
Jansenism—may have been as important as that of Roman law in
leading jurists toward applying divine or natural law to positive
law.)

For L'Hospital, natural law was the invariable rule for personal
conduct. "Let us keep in mind," he said, "that the true law of nature
is not to do to other people what we do not want done to our-
selves."[92] The justice of positive law, as the chancellor described it,
was somewhat more limited and insensible, as it were, than that,
having "regard . . . for that which belongs to other people in order to
distribute it to them."[93] The chancellor suggested that in the latter
respect the law might, at its most sublime, achieve for "the city, the
republic, and the state" the same kind of natural order found in the
godlike soul. "When the parts of the soul are so well regulated and
composed," he said, "that they produce in us prudence, temperance,
[and] magnanimity, these three elements form and establish a very
beautiful and harmonious *justice* in man, which makes him approach the divine nature, when each part of the soul has what belongs to it."[94] The concerted attempt to create that natural order in
the kingdom would have to wait, however, for more favorable times.

Going back a few years, on the eve of the religious wars Jean de
Coras wrote a *Discours des parties et office d'un bon et entier juge*. Five
qualities, he said, were essential to the good and right-minded judge:
age, prudence, experience, erudition, and integrity. Under erudition
he included knowledge of both positive and divine law, and he
stressed the greater importance of knowing the latter. "Of all the
disciplines," he said, "the most necessary is, without question, cognizance of the law of God." He went on to state, "and if the judge
follows thus the law of God and there is someone so . . . arrogant that
he does not want to obey him, that one, said the Lord through the
mouth of Moses, will die, since such who head-strongly resists the
magistrate rebels against God, from whom proceeds all power."[95]
Coras still distinguished between positive and divine law. His magistrate had to study both. While he urged the judge to base his deci-

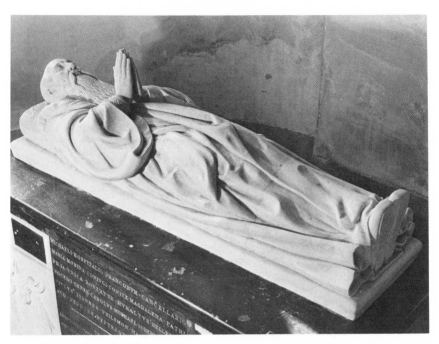

3. *Tomb of Michel L'Hospital.* Chapel at Champmoteux (Seine-et-Oise).

sions on the examples of the justice of God given in the Scriptures, his injunction remained more a personal one, intended to govern the conduct of judges, than a theoretical one, aimed to guide legislators in a reformulation of the laws. His work belonged to a common, sixteenth-century genre of manuals for judges and princes. Their authors meant for the dignitaries to read the manuals and follow the rules of conduct that they set forth.[96] Jacques Labitte's *Règlement pour la réformation et abbréviation de la Iustice du Duché de Mayne et sieges qui en dépendent,* which pointed to professional and disciplinary matters to which attention should be paid if the courts were to run smoothly and regularly, probably took its inspiration from literature of this genre.[97] Labitte made recommendations for specific statutory regulations of conduct.

Coquille, writing in 1573, the year of L'Hospital's death, agreed with Seyssel's and L'Hospital's definitions of justice. He reminds one, though, that *justice,* in another sense of the word, still meant a patrimonial droit. "The first and principal mark of the grandeur of the grandees," he said, "is Justice, which is to say, the right of administering Justice to their subjects. It is that which renders them similar to God and by reason of which in the Scripture, in one manner of speaking, they are called gods, and by the poets are called heroes and demigods, sired by God."[98] As early as 1539, Charles Dumoulin had dissociated *fief* and *justice,* saying that the two had nothing in common.[99] In the early seventeenth century, Loyseau, too, challenged the notion of justice as patrimony, saying that "patrimonial . . . has always had another sense in Justice than in fief." He seems not to have meant, however, that justice in general should not be patrimonial, but that it was properly the patrimony of the king alone: "the *droit de ressort* is plainly one of the rights of the crown; that is why it is called by its true name, *droit de Souveraineté.*"[100]

Bodin, in his work of 1576–1584, also stated his desire for the integration of positive and natural law. "The law of the prince," he said, "should be framed unto the modell of the law of God."[101] He defined *justice* in nearly the same way as L'Hospital, declaring: "Justice therefore I say to be *The right division of rewards and punishments, and of that which of right unto every man belongeth.*"[102] He advocated "Harmonicall" justice, a mixture of the distributive, or "Geometricall," justice typical of aristocratic states and the commutative, or "Arithmeticall," justice typical of popular states. For, he wrote, "these two proportions of Arithmeticall and Geometricall government, the one governing by law onely, and the other by discretion without any law at all, do ruinat and destroy estates and Commonweales: but being by Harmonicall proportion compounded and combined together, serve well to preserve and maintaine the same."[103] "Harmonicall" justice, which to Bodin approximated the law of God, was the happy conjuncture of the characteristics of a certain kind of state—namely, monarchy.[104] It was the result of a well-designed mechanism, with a king at its center who bound himself "more straitly" than his subjects to the law of God and nature. Other, inferior kinds of justice were the modes of other types of political organization.

But Bodin saw that monarchies were not always all that they should be. Furthermore, he knew that others also saw that. He hedged his work about with warnings against revolt. He did, though, state conditions under which a foreign prince, or perhaps any foreigner, might call an erring king to account. For he was not confident that monarchies, even with the best devised laws, would always keep from becoming tyrannies.[105]

Loyseau, in defining *justice*, similarly emphasized one's obligation toward it. "It is," he said, "the unique end of justice and the office of the judge also to attribute to each one that which belongs to him: and that is not called giving but rendering; it is not gratuity but duty."[106] In his synthesis of Roman and natural law, Domat restated that this, no ordinary duty, was a judge's divine duty.

Domat partook not only of the influence of Saint Augustine, which came to him through Jansenism, but also of something new, which set him apart from the jurists of the sixteenth and early seventeenth centuries—namely, the spirit of modern reform. It was this spirit that led him, quite consciously and explicitly, to search out the simplest and most basic premises of the law—which his Jansenist leanings insured would be the principles of natural law—and to build up from them a clear, systematic, and unified law. It was this spirit that imbued him with the confidence to proceed from the point where others had stopped and actually to set forth his desired reforms in full detail, favorable times or not. His statement of method could have been taken almost verbatim from Descartes. "One intends," said Domat in the preface to his *Les loix civiles dans leur ordre naturel*, in which he took it upon himself to explain the "design" of his work, something that writers had seldom felt obliged to meditate upon:

two principal effects from this order: brevity, from the elimination of the useless and superfluous; and clarity, by the simple effect of the arrangement. And one has hoped that by this brevity and this clarity, it would be easy to learn the laws thoroughly and in little time, and even that the study of them, becoming easy, would be agreeable. Since as the truth is the natural object of the mind of man, it is the sight of the truth that brings him pleasure; and this pleasure is greater in proportion that the truths are more natural to our reason, and that our reason sees them in their light without difficulty . . . Some of those who will read this book may be surprised to find in several places therein truths so common and so easy that it will appear to them of no utility to state them, since no one is unaware of them. But they could learn from those who know the sciences that it is by these sorts of truths, so simple and so self-evident, that one comes to the understanding of those that are less so, and that for the detailed account of a science it is necessary to collect them all and to form the whole corpus, which should be composed of their assemblage. Hence, in geometry it is necessary to begin by learning that the whole is greater than any of its parts, that two areas equal to a third are equal to each other, and other truths that children know, but the employment of which is necessary in order to penetrate to others, less evident, and several so profound that all minds are not capable of reaching them.[107]

While Domat called for the introduction of modern methods in legal studies, others urged their adoption by all disciplines. "The geometric spirit," said Fontenelle, in a famous passage, "is not so attached to geometry that it cannot be taken from it and transported to other subjects of understanding. A work on ethics, on politics, of criticism, perhaps even of eloquence, will be for it finer, all other things being equal, if it is fashioned by the hand of the geometer."[108] By the middle of the eighteenth century, specific acknowledgments of the new method had mostly disappeared from non-scientific and philosophical works. D'Aguesseau was one of the last of the reformers to be considered here to refer, for instance, to Descartes as his inspiration. To d'Aguesseau, Descartes "had invented the art of making use of reason."[109] But the absence of further references indicates, in this case, only that the modern approach to reform had become, for many, habitual and hence unremarkable.

In the second manifestation of a modern approach to judicial reform, one may see that the emphasis of reform changed between the sixteenth and the second half of the seventeenth century. Reforms of the sixteenth century were concerned with the appellate or jurisdictional organization of the courts and, to a lesser degree, with procedure and discipline.[110] The important reforms of the later seventeenth century had more to do with the internal organization of courts. As in, most notably, the work of Colbert's commissions of the 1660s, which culminated in the Ordonnance civile of 1667 and the Ordonnance criminelle of 1670, they also placed much more emphasis on procedure.[111] The desire for this penetrating, severe kind of judicial reform appeared, for example, in the work that Abbé Claude Fleury addressed to his student, the duke of Burgundy: "La réforme de l'administration."

Fleury recommended drastic reductions in the number of officers and elimination of "useless" jurisdictions; the reformation of French criminal procedure; open civil proceedings; and more careful monitoring by the intendants of all judicial activities in the provinces. Fleury did not recommend an end either to the venality of offices in general or to épices. He did not have the full measure of modern optimism with respect to the possibility of reform. But he did urge the crown to see that criminal cases where there was no civil party would not go untried because there was no one to pay the judges. In these situations, he said, the crown should provide the judges with their fees. And he also urged that special courts for the privileged be abolished and that "great crimes in all persons, without exception," be punished. It was necessary, he stated, to "remedy abuses not in particulars by small regulations, but in retracing [them] to the source."[112]

To L'Hospital and others for whom *justice* meant giving to each person what belonged to him, it made sense to have one kind of court to specialize in giving one sort of claimant his due and another kind for giving another sort his due. Nor did jurists in the sixteenth century, who suffered no apparent discomfort from using the word *justice* in various senses, feel uncomfortable with many kinds of courts, vaguely or illogically differentiated from each other and diversely constituted.

During the seventeenth century such confusion became intolerable to jurists applying new functional, aesthetic, and moral standards to the laws and courts. Rather than adding to the courts, the modern jurists turned their attention inward, scrutinized the existing institutions, and tried to make them work better. These later jurists viewed *justice* comprehensively. It made sense to them therefore to have a single hierarchy of courts, competent in all or nearly all matters. Domat distinguished, basically, between "natural and necessary procedures" and those that were the result "of the passion of the parties or of the malversation of those who have a hand in the prosecution of justice." "To determine, then," said Domat, "that which there is of the natural and essential in the judicial order and to discern by this understanding that which one mixes there of the vicious and superfluous, it is necessary to scour the natural order, the justice and the truth of which, one should make the judges understand."[113] It was thus that Domat would have expedited justice: not by the further elaboration of institutions but by their simplification and by bringing their conduct into conformity with what he considered the single universal norm.

Finally, in the third manifestation of its influence, the modern reforming method did give some of its proponents an optimism about reform unheard of among traditional reformers. In at least one case, the optimism expressed itself in utopianism. Géraud de Cordemoy, who was both a fervent Cartesian and a devotee of Plato, used the device in his utopian program for the administration of justice, *De la réformation d'un état,* of having himself meet the ambassador of a distant land. The ambassador tells Cordemoy that the young king of his country has just reformed the state from top to bottom and given it perfect laws. Cordemoy related what the ambassador told him about this imaginary country and its new order.

Cordemoy envisioned a society of people so well brought up and educated that they would hardly ever have disputes requiring adjudication. "Better judges without cases," he said, "than cases without judges." To settle cases that did arise, the king would send out a *président* every two years who would appoint a judge in each city from names with which a *procureur général* would provide him. The procureur général would be elected, also every two years, by assemblies of the notables of each locale. The judge so appointed would hold court every day and in such an efficient way that the "greatest pettyfoggers" would not be able to keep a trial going more than three days. There would be neither épices nor legal fees. Both judges and lawyers would be paid regularly every quarter, in advance, by the crown. All positions would be held by royal appointment or local election; none would be purchased. Cities would be divided, for all purposes, into districts as nearly equal as possible. In all other respects, too—except in its essential monarchical form of government and in the organization of the Church, both of which Cordemoy stepped lightly around—France was to be made into a *tabula rasa* and constructed anew, according to a different plan.[114]

As a final thought before ending this chapter, it might be worthwhile to speculate on the reasons that modern reformers found for disregarding the warnings of the philosopher, Descartes, from whom some of them claimed to receive their impetus. One might argue that Descartes was usually more sanguine about the results of his inquiries than he admitted. As was well known, he died before he completed his work. He had perhaps planned to use his method to produce a system of ethics.[115] His followers might have been able to visualize yet grander designs of his without much difficulty. A broader explanation, though, might emphasize the general ebullience in scientific and other learned circles during the seventeenth century over the immense amount of knowledge being added to the inheritance from the ancients in an unprecedentedly short time and the resulting feeling that remaining problems of all types could be solved.

## 2 / Objectives of Judicial Reform in the Eighteenth Century

A dialectical tension between traditional and modern reform played itself out in France during the eighteenth century. The works in the first half of the century of the Abbé de Saint-Pierre, Chancellor d'Aguesseau, and the Marquis d'Argenson, which introduced, between them, all the themes of court reform in that century, showed evidence of this tension and at the same time an ignorance of the need for its resolution. An examination of the works of these three reformers is also instructive because of the thoughts that they recorded on each other's work, which provide an idea of the kind of dialogue out of which the different works grew.

### Saint-Pierre, the Utility of Laws, and the Supremacy of Law over Custom

The Abbé de Saint-Pierre believed that social ills could be ended and social benefits achieved through legislation. The effects of laws were certain and predetermined, and so one could calculate what the utility of the laws would be. Perhaps no one before Saint-Pierre had so unequivocally preferred law to custom or been so confident that law, if it were well enough written, could prevail. Because the legislator, in the mind of Saint-Pierre, was able to foresee the consequences of his acts, he could produce more good for society than would ever result from the meanderings of custom. He could cut short the developments of centuries and set in motion new developments that he thought would be more beneficial. The effects of law had the predictability of mathematics or machinery; a law set off a sequence of causes and effects that followed logically, one from another.

In his *Mémoire pour diminuer le nombre des procès*, Saint-Pierre occupied himself with the springs of litigation in France. "The undertaking that I have the honor of proposing in this work to your majesty," said the abbé in the dedication of his treatise to the new king, Louis XV, "is ... to diminish very considerably between the

families of your subjects the prodigious numbers of lawsuits, which
are sorts of civil wars between citizens."[1] He divided his work into
two parts. In the first he proposed that the king set up an academy
to improve and codify French law. In the second he described some
of the means by which the number of lawsuits could be decreased.

The means that he listed in the second part were: (1) reducing to
one degree all jurisdictions below the parlements; (2) making uniform the size and clarifying the limits of jurisdictions; (3) augment-
ing the competency of the présidiaux; (4) specializing the *chambres*
("divisions") of the law courts in different sorts of cases; (5) recognizing superior judges by allowing them two votes instead of one; (6)
remedying the ill effects of, though not abolishing, the venality of

4. *Charles-Irénée Castel, l'abbé de Saint-Pierre,* by Maurice-Quentin de La Tour.

judicial offices; (7) reducing the number of *jugements d'Audience* and increasing proportionately the number of *jugements par Raporteur* (that is, requiring lawyers more often to write out their arguments and deliver them to a person appointed by the court as a reporter rather than letting the lawyers present their arguments orally before the judges); (8) requiring approval by two experienced lawyers before any subpoena be issued; (9) strictly enforcing laws providing for the security of the public, particularly with respect to embezzlement, theft, and assassination; (10) freeing persons imprisoned for debts under a certain amount, along the lines of a recent (1724) reform in English law; (11) requiring clerks and public copyists to write court writs and other documents legibly; (12) establishing a public depository for the records of notaries so that those whom the records concerned could easily consult them; and (13) making laws regarding entails uniform throughout the kingdom. In an addendum, Saint-Pierre reflected on ways to improve the public law of Germany, or the law common to all the German states.

The abbé's proposals were sketchy, tentative, and uncorrelated. In another work, after recommending the creation of more parlements and the replacement of venal by elective judgeships, Saint-Pierre apologized, "I see well that this is neither demonstrated nor gone deeply into: these are only political fragments, which should be considered only as materials worthy of being examined."[2] Surely the same apology would have been appropriate here. But the abbé was impatient to show what his proposed reforms would accomplish. For his concern with the judiciary was only a facet of his concern for society and the international community. He wanted judicial reforms because of the widespread effects they would have. The expedition of justice, which was the object of all the court reforms that he suggested, would, he believed, result in great benefits for France and the rest of Europe.

First of all, lawsuits cost the people of France many "difficulties, anxieties, afflictions, losses, and expenses." So a decrease in the number and length of lawsuits would relieve the people of a corresponding number of their troubles.[3] Second, the addition to the political economy of the time, labor, and wealth that would no longer be consumed by legal actions would boost the commerce of the nation. Third, the state would realize an increase in revenue from the expansion of commerce.[4] And finally, lawsuits, which Saint-Pierre likened to warfare within the state, created unrest that could spill over into the relations between France and other states and thus endanger international peace. Hence the fewer the lawsuits, the weaker the threat to peace.[5]

Except perhaps for the last one, none of these general objectives of judicial reform was new. Where Saint-Pierre's work showed a difference was in its attempt at a systematic demonstration of how the objectives would be achieved. The abbé went so far, indeed, as to calculate the amount of money that a diminution of lawsuits would add to commerce and thence to the king's treasury. "It is not that I do not see," he said,

that one can dispute with me the foundations of my calculation and that one cannot prove that I am mistaken, be it by too much, be it by too little; but it is nevertheless true that in the matter of politics, if one wants to give more precise ideas and to make comparisons of different resolutions with more accuracy, it is of an indispensable necessity to bring all arguments down to a sort of calculation of revenue, because as imperfect as this calculation is, the mind of the reader finds itself greatly relieved and pronounces with much more certitude not only whether one decision is better than another, but yet of how much it is the better.[6]

By way of showing how much better the enactment of his proposals would make life in France, Saint-Pierre let one suppose that the academy he proposed was set up and that it succeeded in bringing the law of the whole kingdom just to the degree of perfection that the decisions of Guillaume de Lamoignon had given to the civil laws of Paris. There would be 365,000 fewer procès ("proceedings") per year in France, with a minimum savings of 73,500,000 livres, "without counting the ordeals of travel, the anxieties of judgments, and the chagrins of losing" that people would be spared. This money, put into commerce and the improvement of land, would considerably enhance the wealth of the state. Then suppose, he said, that the academy was even more successful and through its work reduced procès by three-fourths over twenty years. Among other advantages of this reduction, the number of judicial officers would shrink by one-half. Those who would ordinarily seek judicial office would go instead into science or commerce, "an occupation more profitable for them and for the state than that of justice, where the profit and the activity are everyday declining."[7]

Also striking in the work of Saint-Pierre was the abbé's unquestioning faith in the efficacy of law. There was, in his mind, no exter-

nal reason for laws not to work. Any fault was in the laws themselves. "I hear it said sometimes," he stated, " 'We have enough good
laws in France, it is only a matter of executing them well', and me, I
say, that we have not enough of them, or that they are not good
enough, inasmuch as these laws have not provided sufficiently for
their execution."[8]

To write laws "concerning the execution of the law," Bodin had
said, was folly, because such laws only provided more opportunities
for litigants and their attorneys to initiate suits and for judges to
prolong trials.[9] Saint-Pierre, however, took a more positive view of
laws and believed that they could cover all potential conflicts between people. Legislation should therefore, he suggested, be ex-
panded to govern every aspect of life. The perfection of the law, to
be sure, would take time. But it could be achieved, and as the law
progressed, lawsuits would become fewer and shorter.[10] The abbé
did not share Bodin's conservatism or his doubts that law could
change custom, and he did not even consider the possibility that
Frenchmen had developed, as Bodin observed, the ability to raise
points of law even out of wholly unambiguous statutes.

Saint-Pierre's contemporary, d'Aguesseau, criticized him in the
same way that Bodin might have for his old and discredited, omnibus approach to drafting legislation. "By what whim," he asked,
"does the Abbé de Saint-Pierre want to extend the laws instead of
reducing them, to add articles to each title of our customs instead of
removing some from them; and is it to be imagined that procès will
diminish in proportion to the additions that one will make to the
laws, instead of thinking that such great detail can furnish as many
occasions for starting procès as means of ending them?"[11] One could
say that the abbé's work showed the first and the third of the manifestations of modern reformism—that is, the systematic referral of
all laws and institutions to a principle of justice (in this case, that
justice should "augment the general good of society")[12] and the confidence or optimism about reform—but not always the second of
them, the tendency to consolidate or rationalize laws and institutions. (D'Aguesseau's work, as will be seen, contained the first and
second of these manifestations but not the third.)

A vestige of another tradition in the work of Saint-Pierre was the
abbé's couching of each of his proposals in Thomist form. He stated

his proposal and explained what its enactment would accomplish, then gave objections that had been raised or that might be raised, and finally replied to each objection in turn. The strength of the Thomist presentation, noted another contemporary of Saint-Pierre's, the Marquis d'Argenson (in criticizing what he would, in another place, term a "bad book"[13] and in explaining why it failed to convince its readers), was in the fullness of the objections and the adequacy of the replies. Unfortunately, d'Argenson went on to say, Saint-Pierre's objections occasionally struck readers as incomplete, and some of his replies struck them as inadequate. When the objections and replies were, on the other hand, too thorough, the Thomist argument seemed pedantic. In the view of d'Argenson, the abbé was also guilty of such pedantry.[14] The incongruity of Saint-Pierre's tedious and archaic presentation with his concise, self-consciously modern statistics, and his use of a mode of argument employed originally to suggest the truth of highly abstract and subtle theological doctrines in order to "demonstrate" the desirability of one or another practical choice in very mundane affairs, may also have dismayed early eighteenth-century readers.

Both the reforms proposed by Saint-Pierre and the abbé's methods of propounding them were thus a mixture of the traditional and the modern. Possibly as a result, his reforms seemed unworkable and his arguments debatable. But the works of his two critical contemporaries d'Aguesseau and d'Argenson also showed unresolved difficulties and were hardly more successful in their immediate impact.

## The Unfulfilled Projects of the Chancellor d'Aguesseau

In 1725, the same year that Saint-Pierre published the second edition of his *Mémoire pour diminuer le nombre des procès*, Henri-François d'Aguesseau wrote his "Mémoire sur les vues générales que l'on peut avoir pour la réformation de la justice."[15] In this work, he proposed unifying French law, reordering the jurisdictions of courts, improving procedure, and supervising more closely the conduct of judicial officers. Some of d'Aguesseau's aims were achieved; encouraged by Cardinal Fleury, the chancellor wrote ordonnances on gifts (*donations*), wills (*testaments*), and entails (*substitutions*). He also embarked on the reform of the lower royal courts, getting the intendants to make a survey of their officials and learning what he could of their actual state. During most of the period of Fleury's government, how-ever—and afterward, too—the crown was preoccupied with foreign affairs. D'Aguesseau, for his part, was often chary of pushing for his reforms. Nevertheless, his long chancellorship marked a significant broadening and deepening of the dialogue on reform in eighteenth-century France.

During his discussion of the ordonnances composed by Colbert's reform commissions, d'Aguesseau said that although the work of the commissions was admirable, it was neither as good nor as successful as one might have hoped. "Their principal aim," he said, "in the Ordonnance civile was to shorten the length of procedures, to make preliminary investigations [*instructions*] simpler, and to diminish fees, but the result has not met their expectations. One has seen on the contrary, since the Ordonnance of 1667, procedures multiplying every day, preliminary investigations being from them only more charged with points of law and objections, and the fees from trials growing instead of diminishing."[16] The reasons why the work of the commissions had the opposite effects from those intended were two-fold, d'Aguesseau believed. In the first place, it had been willfully subverted. "The subtlety and the malice of men," stated the Jansen-ist-influenced d'Aguesseau, "nearly always go further . . . than the foresight of the legislator."[17] Second, the work had not penetrated to the roots of problems in the administration of justice—namely, "the mixture of finance with justice," the existence of multitudinous of-fices, and the practice of collecting fees for various court services.

The chancellor's second point was almost identical to a point made by L'Hospital in the sixteenth century. His first point, too, could have been made by a sixteenth-century Frenchman. In d'Aguesseau, indeed, one sees how Jansenism, while it had contrib-uted to the belief of some jurists that natural law should be the basis of civil life and institutions and had thus helped formulate an axiom from which to construct geometrically a new set of laws and courts, had also dampened modern optimism that such a reconstruction could be achieved. Where d'Aguesseau diverged from his traditional predecessors, though, was in his distinct preference for law over cus-tom and his consequent tendency toward reform rather than conser-vation. His Jansenist orientation did not allow him to be optimistic

Illi Lingua potens Demofthenis, Ars Ciceronis,
   Pectus Ariftidis, Mensque Platonis erat:
Et Cato Cenfurâ, Refpontis Papinianus,
   Comiliis Neftor, Legibus ipfe Solon.
Verior his Virtus animo labrisque fedebat,
   Ipfa etiam Scriptis nunc quoque vifa loqui.

5. *Henri-François d'Aguesseau at the Age of Thirty-five.* Engraving by J. Daullé
(1761) from a painting by Joseph Vivien (1703).

about reform like his freethinking clerical acquaintance Saint-Pierre. But he did share the abbé's belief in the superior wisdom of the legislator.

"All good legislation," said d'Aguesseau, in another work on judicial reform, "should be systematic and act always in a consistent manner."[18] His working model was Domat, who had been one of his teachers, and it was Domat's modern sense of order that the chancellor principally admired. Domat's sense of order, in d'Aguesseau's opinion, had been superior even to Tribonian's. "Though the arrangement of the Institutes of Justinian is not defective," he stated, "more than once one would have hoped that this arrangement had been made by Domat instead of Tribonian."[19] And the superiority of laws arranged and fixed "scientifically" over disorganized and indefinite or fluctuating customs was, in the mind of the chancellor, incontestable.[20]

Like some other eighteenth-century Frenchmen, d'Aguesseau saw his ideal in ancient Sparta. The orderliness of its laws corresponded to what he wanted for France, and he compared Sparta favorably with all other states as well. "It was not without reason," he said,

that Lycurgus believed that laws that only remedied particular disadvantages produced hardly any effect and were nearly always without utility . . . [Because most laws are like that], there is hardly any kingdom or republic where one sees a true and perfect legislation. Governing rules establish themselves almost as cities are built: there is no plan nor general system. Chance, conjunctures, at the very most some reflections of a wise man or the belated lessons of experience produce a great number of laws or particular regulations. . . .

It is yet much worse in the states that last for a great number of centuries. The legislation is like an old building, always on the verge of ruin, that is necessary to prop up or repair on every side; and because there would be too much to do, one does nothing at all. Sparta is maybe the only republic which had a true body of legislation, composed of a small number of laws, but all related to the common good, all efficacious, and all effectively executed.[21]

To achieve "a solid and durable reform" in France, "a true reform of the excess of procedures," d'Aguesseau said that one must go to "la source du mal," to the preconditions for the ills of justice. One must reduce the number of court officers, suppress a large portion of the fees that they collect, and establish a stricter discipline in the courts. L'Hospital, too, had seen little chance of success for procedural or organizational reforms unless disciplinary and structural problems were first attended to. D'Aguesseau's approach to those problems, however, showed modern aspects lacking in the recommendations of the sixteenth-century chancellor. In his discussion, for instance, of the assizes held by bailliages to hear people's complaints against seignorial and other inferior justices, d'Aguesseau urged a systematic, internal reform of the institution, "dividing the ressort of each bailliage into several departments, in each of which there would be a certain number of justices who would respond to the assize, which one would hold in a place that would be like the common center of justice." And in his proposal to abolish the sale of a few principal offices in each of the royal courts, d'Aguesseau suggested that a simple, annual levy be made on each locality to cover the costs of reimbursing the holders of those offices. The appointees who would be installed in the key positions would be "honorable and disinterested" and would set an example for the rest of the officers.[22]

Many of the reforms that the chancellor proposed were still, as the chancellor himself averred, quite traditional. They would have restored institutions to what they had been in an earlier and, in the view of d'Aguesseau, better time. "Nothing would be more useful," he said, "for making justice truly flourish in this realm than the frequent use of *grands jours* [extraordinary assizes where all crimes were exposed in 'broad daylight'] . . ." *Mercuriales* (reopening sessions of courts of law at which the premier président gave a speech denouncing abuses in the courts), according to d'Aguesseau, should also be revived, not as the occasions for "pure oratory" to which they had degenerated, but as the occasions for moral reprimanding of the judges that they had been in the time of L'Hospital. "It is a question, then, in this regard," said the chancellor, "of reestablishing some laws already made and which should always have been inviolably observed."[23] But such reestablishments were most often to take place on new foundations.

The most striking combination of traditional and modern approaches appeared in d'Aguesseau's project for reforming the lower royal courts: the présidiaux; bailliages and sénéchaussées; and prévôts, vicomtes, châtelains, and viguiers. Noting "with sadness" the decline of these courts, the "nearly general disgust" with offices in them—a disgust that had replaced the "nearly incredible avidity" with which the offices had formerly been sought—the chancellor wrote to the intendants in 1740, asking their assistance. He requested that the intendants solicit the views of members of courts in their *généralités* and make their own recommendations about what might be done to renovate the courts. Detailed questionnaires accompanied the letters. The exact state of each tribunal was to be determined so that one could devise "the most convenient means for establishing the best order possible in this part of the administration of justice and for restoring prestige to the offices there in the ways least onerous to the king, the public, and the officers."[24]

The emphasis of the chancellor's project was on restoring old institutions; he did not contemplate creating new ones. In formulating his reasons for undertaking especially the reform of the présidiaux, however, d'Aguesseau revealed that the reformed courts he envisioned were not quite the same as the ones set up in 1551–1552. "Although the public good had been to a certain extent the object of the edicts creating the présidiaux," he said, in treating the courts that seemed to be in the most immediate need of attention, "it is necessary to acknowledge that reasons of finance had yet more of a hand there than the motives of pure justice."[25] In his view, only the shadow, not the substance, of good intentions had been present at the creation of the présidiaux. He went on to show how the courts could be remade so that the service of the *bien public* ("common welfare") would truly be the basis of their establishment.

The first and most important step, in the chancellor's mind, toward remaking the présidial jurisdiction so that it would function in the public interest was to reduce by half the number of bailliages and sénéchaussées designated as having the additional, présidial competence. Only in this way could the remaining présidiaux be strengthened sufficiently to fulfill the expectations that the chancellor had of them. Hence d'Aguesseau, in his survey of the intendants, asked for advice regarding which présidiaux should be suppressed or combined with other présidiaux. (It was, indeed, one of the chancellor's general aims to reduce the number of courts and with them the degrees of jurisdiction. While his program for paring the number of présidiaux was never carried out, he did succeed, between 1734 and 1749, in abolishing nearly all the prévôts, vicomtes, châtelains, and viguiers—the lowest royal courts—in towns where there were also bailliages or sénéchaussées, thus effectively reducing royal justice to two degrees in many areas.)

D'Aguesseau's reformed présidiaux would not only have been fewer in number but would also have had their ressorts augmented to bring them in line with inflated prices. They would have been shown other considerations as well, such that they would have attracted "the most distinguished subjects in the provinces."[26] One can indeed imagine a system of super-présidiaux, something like the grands bailliages of Lamoignon in 1788, that would have challenged the parlements and redirected the flow of judicial business in the kingdom.[27] In suggesting this new system, d'Aguesseau revealed most clearly that despite his respect for and identification with the parlements he saw that their bloated size and importance did not make for the most efficient justice nor serve the best interests of the people.[28]

The peculiar weakness of d'Aguesseau's traditional and modern program was that it provoked opposition not only from the parlements, which had always opposed any strengthening of the courts beneath them (and which were institutionally and temperamentally even less able to accommodate themselves to chancellor d'Aguesseau's program), but also from the very courts, the présidiaux, that it was intended to serve. No présidial, no matter how moribund, wanted to be eliminated, at least at this early date. A recent historian has said that the "pronounced competitive character" of the institutions of Old Regime France tended always to undo partial or gradual reforms, while the crown lacked the will, stamina, and social authority required for radical reform.[29] Moreover, the piecemeal reforms—which belong with those reforms here called traditional—were almost always mixed in the eighteenth century with radical or modern elements, and this combination of reforms perplexed and disturbed officeholders, often perhaps without their knowing why, and led them to oppose the reforms with more than their usual tenacity. The different parts of the reform programs—their traditional and modern components—likewise often worked at cross-purposes and thus in themselves contributed to the failure of reform. Maupeou's reform, for example, far from being the clearest, most radical, or modern of the reforms attempted before the 1770s by the crown—as many have described it—was rather the most confused of them, the one in which traditional and modern elements were in the most pronounced and hopelessly irreconcilable conflict. Its short-lived success was made possible only by a temporary imbalance of forces at the royal court, in conjunction, perhaps, with a last despotic mood of the stubborn, sporadically forceful Louis XV.

With respect to d'Aguesseau and his efforts at reforming the présidiaux, one can readily see how awkward their combination of traditional and modern objectives was and how that combination made them hardly more desirable than practical. To restore luster to présidial offices in order to reverse the desertion of them by the judicial bourgeoisie was the chancellor's ostensibly traditional goal; to found the courts anew on the principle of public service was his modern ambition. The former he saw as a means to the latter. Offices in consolidated and strengthened présidiaux would once again attract the cream of the legal class, many of whom had been drifting away from the courts in response to other, more lucrative callings; and with a capable officer corps, the *jambe de force* of any administration, justice would be better rendered. The problems with this scheme, unfortunately, were manifold.

Most significantly, the scheme comprised higher professional standards for judicial personnel without the structural reforms—the replacement of proprietary judgeships and the collection of épices with a system of appointed, salaried officers—long regarded as essential to the establishment of such standards. While d'Aguesseau himself recognized that structual problems were largely responsible for the faults in judicial administration, he did not include in his program a plan for correcting them. His approach was rather to control them, as by frequent assizes, the supervision of venal officeholders by appointed chief judges, and the stricter enforcement of an edict of 1673 against certain abuses in the collection of épices.[30] Nor was d'Aguesseau's failure to establish the necessary prerequisites for reform the result simply of his practical recognition that the crown lacked the wherewithal for changing the way that judicial positions were held. Natural law could be interpreted not only to call for the establishment of a fairer, more efficient judiciary but also to support the right of judges to their offices—their property—accompanied by their right to dispose of them only if and when they chose. D'Aguesseau seemed to come down on the side of respect for property.

In 1718–1720, d'Aguesseau had written two memoirs aimed against John Law, part of whose rationale for expanding the money supply had been to provide funds with which the crown could reimburse officeholders for the price of their positions and thus permanently end the venality of offices.[31] In the *Considérations sur les monnaies,* the chancellor argued that gold and silver each had a natural value, which the king had therefore no right to touch, and in his *Mémoire sur le commerce de la Compagnie des Indes* he condemned speculation on the grounds that it was not in accordance with natural justice for one person to enrich himself at the expense of another.[32] While his critical view of Law was probably justified, his reasons for taking that view showed how conservative his belief in natural law had made him and how little, really, he was prepared to change in order to create the conditions in which a more idealistic defense of natural law could flourish.

Within the context of a venal-office holding, épice-collecting judiciary, the public interest would have been served by an improvement in the position of judges only to a point. For a refurbishing of judgeships would have led to an enhancement in their price that would in turn have resulted in an upward trend in court costs to litigants. Those who finally got judicial offices would have wanted to profit from their investments. The modern aim of an organizational revolution would thus very possibly have been subverted by the traditional program of restoring prestige and income to officeholders. The consolidation of courts would have been opposed to the public good to the extent that the burdens of increased travel and increased cost for many litigants would not have been offset by an improvement in the quality of justice received.

Some of the chancellor's ideas for improving the situation of the judges would undoubtedly have been in the interest of the public, too. Most notable in this respect was his suggestion that judicial processes be freed of many of the droits, or taxes (which, in this case, went to the crown, not to the judges), with which they were encumbered.[33] These droits made justice prohibitively expensive for some people. By thus reducing the number of cases coming into the courts, the droits also hurt the judges by reducing the amount of income they could expect from épices. But in general, the renovation of old, proprietary offices and the securing of justice in the public interest were probably contradictory ends.

The fact that the reforms were not enacted possibly made matters worse. For added to the existing insecurities of officeholders was the new fear that in the future the crown might succeed in abolishing or combining some of their jurisdictions. The specter of further reform rising behind the failure of d'Aguesseau's project for the présidiaux may have made lower court offices even less desirable, encouraged their further desertion, and compounded existing ills. But it is difficult to imagine how the reforms might have succeeded.

D'Aguesseau believed that the failure resulted from the king's lack of commitment to the reforms. Certainly the crown did have other preoccupations. In an earlier, characteristically apprehensive statement, the chancellor had said, "I do not know whether one can ever hope, in this kingdom, to succeed in a solid and serious reformation of justice."[34] He shared the common eighteenth-century notion that failures of the state were due primarily to its lack of adequate leadership. Like his sixteenth-century predecessors, he resigned himself to the deferment of reform to a time more "favorable to the execution of so laudable a design."

An aspiring reformer, Barthélemy-Joseph Bretonnier, similarly looked for a visionary leader to set things aright. "Often I have made the wish," said Bretonnier, "that it would please God to send a prophet to Israel, that is to say, a chancellor who had all the qualities necessary to a good legislator: uprightness, clearmindedness, solid judgment, exquisite discernment, profound understanding of Roman law and French jurisprudence, long experience with judicial affairs—who had no other object, no other interest, no other passion, than the love of justice and the public good."[35] In d'Aguesseau himself, Bretonnier professed, France had found such a chancellor. If the ideal chancellor had had the ideal king, however, and also better circumstances, the success of his reforms would still have been very doubtful. For they shared the shortcoming of reforms generally during the eighteenth century. They showed a lack of resolution between the two warring conceptions of reform—the traditional and the modern—in both of which d'Aguesseau, like so many others, had been simultaneously indoctrinated. They were inherently flawed.

D'Aguesseau, in the end, had only tarred himself with the same brush as his acquaintance Saint-Pierre. "The chancellor loves to write laws," their more daring contemporary, the Marquis d'Argenson, disparagingly said of him.[36] Like Saint-Pierre, according to the marquis, the chancellor had wanted to "consider separately each point of difficulty and to apply himself to remedying that before going further." Being an effective legislator, said the marquis, required looking at things on a large scale ("voir en grand"); it required "detaching oneself from that which one knows the best and thus forsaking all the pride that one takes in one's knowledge." D'Aguesseau was a hopelessly myopic *érudit;* a legislator, in d'Argenson's view did not allow himself to get mired in details. D'Aguesseau had faulted the *publiciste* Saint-Pierre for his amateurish, if occasionally inspired, approach to complicated legal issues. The *théoricien* d'Argenson similarly castigated the *juriste* d'Aguesseau for his inability to grasp the political changes necessary before even the best conceived administrative reform could take place.

Saint-Pierre came closer to d'Argenson's heart. To the marquis, Saint-Pierre was, in fact, "a great genius in politics."[37] "This *philosophe*," he said, "profoundly meditated upon and pushed very far a science, the grandest and most useful of all, and which no one understands today: it is political science, not that which consists in finessing above all, in deceiving in negotiations, but that of rendering men happy and the country solidly glorious."[38] But if the abbé's intention had been good, his focus had been misdirected. He had concentrated his attention on separate aspects of the state, not on its essential character. For d'Argenson the only lasting reform would come through the regenerative power of democracy. Add democratic elements to the French monarchy and all else would follow.

### The Marquis d'Argenson and the Association of Judicial Reform with Politics

D'Argenson intended not so much to reform the judiciary as to bypass it. He had ideas for reforming the courts, just as he had ideas for reforming almost all the institutions of Old Regime France. But he devoted his greatest care to his plan for *magistrats populaires,* which he thought would infuse the needed democracy into the French body politic. The magistrats populaires would provide for the essential regeneration of the state, for that "movement of continuity and renewal that augments and perfects itself and that is precisely the reason for the internal flourishing of republics."[39] France, he said,

was "perhaps the only one of the Christian states" in which important police functions, for example, were "entrusted to royal officials
who do not respond to the people." "Admit the public more to the
government of the public," he urged, "and see what happens."[40]

Fearing large assemblies of the public, which he thought were
dangerous, the marquis did not propose reviving the provincial and
national estates that once allowed Frenchmen to participate in the
decisions of the king's government. Instead he proposed that delegates of the people, the magistrats populaires, be established in each
city, town, and village and given the same authority, particularly
with respect to taxation, as the estates. This *morcellement* of the authority of the estates would allow the public to act on its own behalf
and to make its interests known with a "certain amount of independence, but without confusion." As well as approving the amount of
taxes to be collected in their districts, the magistrats were apparently
to supervise their collection; and they were also to be given the responsibilities then in the hands of the judiciary and the intendances
for policing their districts. The communes, he believed, would police
themselves much more efficiently than royal officials policed them,
because their own persons and property would be at stake. The new
structure of internal government that d'Argenson sketched was not
to be hewn with one blow, but was rather to be built "little by little,
in extending the functions and the fullness of authority that one
proposes to give to these magistrats only according to the first suc-
cesses."[41]

The law courts were of a piece with the royal government that
d'Argenson wanted to push back. Their intrusion into the areas of
police and general administration was unwarranted; they were to be
restricted to purely judicial affairs, to "la justice contentieuse." But
likewise the local magistrats were not to interfere with justice, "pro-
visional or feudal, high, middle, or low."[42] Legal questions were to
be decided, just as before, by the royal or seignorial judges. D'Argenson distinguished between the constitution and laws of the state,
which were in the purview of the king and his officials, and regulations concerning the common people, which alone should be the
province of popular representatives.[43] To fill their role more effectively, however, the courts were to be reformed and the laws were to
be greatly simplified. "There is," said the marquis, "only the abro-
gation of useless laws in general, the greater arbitration of the judge,

6. *René-Louis de Voyer, marquis d'Argenson.* Anonymous.

and the honor that one introduces there that will ever remedy the abuses of justice."[44] The venality of judicial offices was also to be abolished.

The "labyrinth" of "useless laws" in which France found itself, "the chaos of rules, constraints, and contradictions" in which "finance, commerce, and even the military" were enveloped, was largely the result, said the marquis, of the role played in the writing of laws by the "gens de Robe," who were served by a certain complexity in the laws.[45] "The character of legislation," he stated, "should be boldness and brevity." "There are countries," he said approvingly, "where the code of laws is so concise that one can read it in a morning."[46] The work of condensing French laws could not be left to the "many small spirits" that had admitted the "hydra" of confusing laws to the French polity in the first place. It must instead be the particular task of a "genius who will reduce things from the compound to the simple"—of, if one will, an enlightened despot. "It is necessary," he said, "to go to the sources and principles of the composition; it is necessary to understand the law of harmony [*droit de convenance*], which is the voice of reason and the source of public happiness: it is necessary to know to prefer it to the rights of titles and even to the right of possession, and in an edifice so grand no one dares to lay the first stone."[47] Like Bretonnier, d'Argenson looked for a leader of great vision and acute intelligence to bring reform, although for the marquis that leader was not Chancellor d'Aguesseau.

More powers of arbitration for the judge would dovetail into the simplification of laws. Because there would presumably be less to dispute in the meaning of the law, one would only need some wise and honest person—the judge—to settle disagreements. The relative success, perhaps, of the commercial courts in France, and possibly also the example of the English justices of the peace, had inspired the marquis to propose this general extension of arbitration.

The most crucial component of a reformed judicial system, however, would be the "honor that one introduces there." Institutional or legal changes could never succeed without an improvement in *moeurs* ("habits or moral practices"). The moeurs of officeholders were the most basic determinant of administrative effectiveness. If on other points he disagreed with d'Aguesseau, on this one he was in accord; and while he found much to admire in Saint-Pierre, on this he and the abbé would most surely have disagreed. For Saint-Pierre it was always the mesh of the net that was not woven closely and tightly enough; for d'Argenson and d'Aguesseau it was the ingenuity of the fish that allowed it to escape. "The abusive subtlety of man," said the marquis, "will always go to infinity to elude rules contrary to his pretensions."[48]

Some improvement in professional conduct could surely be expected from the elimination of the venality of offices, the "miserable invention that has produced all the evil that is to be set upright again and from which escape has become so difficult."[49] The introduction of venality had marked a watershed in French history. It had stopped the progress of democracy, diverting the public power into the hands of a new class of officeholders who were not tied to the communes in which they served and who could not be removed even by the king himself.[50] The decentralization of the Middle Ages had been replaced by the pseudo-decentralization of ensconced local officials. In the eighteenth century, however, the venal regime was winding down. Demand for offices was decreasing. The vitality, or even the continuance on some levels, of the royal administration could seemingly be insured no longer by the sale of offices. It was in this crisis of the venal regime, perhaps, that d'Argenson was able to observe the drawbacks of the regime so clearly and that he saw the opportunity to end it. Unlike d'Aguesseau, he did support John Law.[51] But he presented no plan of his own for ending venality, and as with his reforms in general, he seemed to believe that once the magistrats populaires were established, abuses would give way and reforms would evolve in due course.

The marquis did not even seem to place much importance on the magistrats. It was rather "the progress of universal reason" that would bring France to a happier state. "The world is childlike," he said, "it weans itself, it perfects itself. Barbarity subsides, and the vices that arise from it disappear. Sooner or later virtues will take their place, since they are only the voice of nature and of order. Already crimes of violence and fanaticism fill us with horror. We have seen nearly die out among us . . . drunkenness, sodomy, kidnapping, poisoning, assassinations; manners are becoming gentler."[52] This notion of a softening of manners became quite common in the course of the eighteenth century. In 1781, Joseph-Michel-Antoine Servan would read a *Discours sur le progrès des connoissances humaines en général, de la morale, et de la législation en particulier* before the Academy of Lyon. Like d'Argenson he would see arising a universal recognition of what was wrong and harmful in the Old Regime and would seem to anticipate a reform by consensus, one that would come naturally and inevitably. "That our procedure is a kind of paralysis that impedes all the movements of justice," said Servan, "is today the truth from all mouths; all citizens know it, sense it, and say it."[53]

Unlike Saint-Pierre—who, according to the marquis, originated the idea that reason was winning out—d'Argenson believed that independently improving moeurs made detailed planning unnecessary. Saint-Pierre made specific proposals for legislation, depending on the utility of laws to supply what force moeurs yet lacked. D'Argenson thought that one would do better to wait for the advance of moeurs, signified by the appearance of an enlightened despot and aided by the democratic magistrats.

D'Argenson's vision of a spontaneously generated, irrepressible spirit of reform that would gradually subdue man's greed and malice separated him from the introspective d'Aguesseau. His perception of the force and self-sufficiency and inimitability of this spirit likewise differentiated the marquis from the social-engineering Saint-Pierre. The reforming spirit would transform the corrupt institutions of the old state without one's having to deal with them directly. It was a question only of recognizing and facilitating the movements of that spirit. Judicial reform would thus neither precede nor lead to any other type of reform or social and economic development, but would occur at the same time.

Insofar as he explained what his new state would be like, d'Argenson seemed to suggest that the king would legislate and the people would regulate, rather the reverse of our democracy, in which executive agencies regulate the application of laws drawn up and passed by representatives of the people. More idealistic than practical, d'Argenson did not foresee the problems that could arise from the fragmentation of regulatory authority. How effective would the new laws of the enlightened despot be? What would happen if the progress of moeurs was uneven in the different parts of the country? Would not the uniform system of justice, the strong, well-disciplined network of courts, be dependent on clear directives and supervision

from a modern, centralized state? D'Argenson's union of a modern
program for radically changing the judiciary with a traditional one
for restoring the fiercely independent communes of the Middle Ages
was one of the most striking examples of the unstable combination
of traditional and modern reform in the eighteenth century.

The confusion in d'Argenson's proposals became even greater as
his perspective and political position shifted. Wanting originally to
restrict the parlements to purely judicial matters and to keep their
members at all costs from writing laws, he came to compare the
Parlement of Paris to the Roman senate, seeing it as the only bul-
wark against the incompetence of Louis XV and his ministers.[54] In
the 1730s when d'Argenson seems to have written his *Considérations
sur le gouvernement ancien et présent de la France,* Louis was young and
was "le bien aimé"; it was still possible for the marquis to see in him
an enlightened ruler. But in the 1750s, at the end of the marquis'
life, the king had matured and the marquis had long since decided
that Louis was not the "genius who will reduce things from the
compound to the simple." Besides having watched the nation suffer
under the rule of this king, however, the marquis had also had hu-
miliating personal experiences in the royal government. These personal experiences may have been the more decisive ones. There
would certainly seem to have been no theoretical justification for
transferring his hopes to the parlementaires—whom he described as
constituting one of the retrograde, privileged orders that had a
vested interest in the Old Regime and no interest at all in reform.

During the rest of the eighteenth century, personal or group
struggles would often take place beneath the banners of opposing
political principles. D'Argenson was only the first to connect judicial
reform, or lack of it, with politics. Notwithstanding its inconsisten-
cies, however, the marquis' work, following as it did upon the work
of Saint-Pierre, also announced the emergence of serious, unofficial
reform literature. While this unofficial literature would never di-
verge completely from royal reform programs, it would comment
more and more critically on them. Rousseau, for example, in his
constitutional projects for Corsica and Poland would suggest that
the only way the crown could make judges more responsible to the
public was to make them part of the public. That is, there should be
no judicial bourgeoisie or caste; instead everyone should take his
turn at being judge for short, fixed terms. To the extent that some-

one did pursue a strictly legal career, he should be put under constant pressure to perform well enough to be promoted to a higher position. Honor should not be gained from staying in one place, but only from acquitting oneself so well there that one was qualified to move ahead.[55] If the monarchy desired an effective judiciary, Rousseau was saying, it was still very far from taking all the steps necessary to build one.

The motives of reformers varied, of course, and were often ulterior to a desire for an improvement in justice for its own sake. The crown was alternately concerned in the eighteenth century with improving the lot of the judicial bourgeoisie in order to maintain the courts and hence that portion of its authority that was still dependent on them and with stopping the challenge to its authority that the courts posed. Other reformers were sometimes concerned with preserving the judiciary to insure a check on royal authority. On another level, however, the works of reformers espoused common objectives. In all the works, for example, of Saint-Pierre, d'Aguesseau, and d'Argenson, one sees a continuation of Domat's attempt to reestablish justice on the basis of natural law by going, in modern reforming fashion, "to the sources and principles of the composition" (d'Argenson) and changing them if necessary to produce the results desired. At the same time, one sees equated with this fundamental change traditional legislative attempts at merely patching up surface problems and even more obviously traditional efforts to return to some supposedly purer state in the past. Interwoven with these objectives were the themes of reviving the présidiaux, redrawing the jurisdictions of the parlements, remedying the abuses of seignorial justice, codifying the laws, reducing the size of the judicial bourgeoisie, and ending the sale of offices. These specific proposals for reform were so often inadequate because they were devised to meet inconsistent objectives.

# 3 / New Directions in Royal Programs for Court Reform

During the sixteenth and seventeenth centuries, the crown had hit the courts with one disciplinary measure and financial obligation after another, but in the eighteenth century no longer took its judiciary for granted. In the eighteenth century, the crown was concerned that the subordination of the judiciary might have been overdone in previous centuries, especially during the reign of Louis XIV, and that the judiciary, particularly on its lower, sub-parlementary levels, might have become too weak to fulfill its functions.

The weakness of the judiciary had other causes as well, which ran deeper than royal interference. Apart from Versailles and the glittering prizes there that were still avidly sought, the entire venal regime was in a profound crisis that the crown may have compounded but had not created. The growth of trade and industry had created many more opportunities for private investment than had previously existed. The "world of merchandise," which the office-seekers of the seventeenth century had regarded with such indifference, now appeared to an increasing number of Frenchmen to hold positive attractions.

Gone was the "Archomanie," or furor for offices, that an early seventeenth-century writer had described: "the more one demands from those who die, the more haste there is to make the king one's heir; the more one investigates officers, the more one searches for offices; the more hazard there is, the more boldly one hazards it; the more that money is rare, the more of it one puts there to perdition; the less there is to occupy oneself in offices, the more one prefers offices to other activities: In brief, the more offices there are, the more rush there is to seek them."[1] Instead there was the "nearly general disgust" for many offices that d'Aguesseau noted. No longer was there a desire for offices that seemingly defied the law of supply and demand and all other laws. Rather there was an appraisal of offices that found many of them wanting. Large numbers of offices that fell to its *parties casuelles,* the crown could not resell, and those that it did sell often went for significantly lower prices.

State offices did not wholly lose their appeal to Frenchmen, and in the nineteenth century, the competition for such positions would again be very keen.[2] But a large part of the old appeal had been that offices were prudent and relatively secure economic and social investments, the colorful theory of an Archomanie notwithstanding, and that they were about the only ones. In the eighteenth century, offices lacked much of that portion of their appeal.

In his purview as supervisor of the French judiciary, the lower courts of ordinary jurisdiction seemed to Chancellor d'Aguesseau to be in special need of attention. D'Aguesseau saw a very real deterioration in these jurisdictions. He also had, however, a modern reforming conception of a consolidated judiciary and some ideas of how the lower courts might be remade to fit into it. The answers that the chancellor received to his survey of 1740 showed, oddly enough, a desire also on the part of some respondents for more than a traditional program of restoring the courts.

Historians have usually emphasized the wide disparity of the replies to the survey of 1740 and to a subsequent one in 1763. They have explained it by saying that a multitude of local, particularist interests and interjurisdictional rivalries and an uneven decline of the courts between one place and another resulted in different perceptions of what needed to be done to improve the situation of the courts.[3] But perhaps the different conceptions of reform that guided the writers of the memorials should be considered instead. The resulting confusion in the memorials put the chancellor at a loss to work out from them a consistent program for reforming the courts. The confusion reflected the chancellor's own and resulted in the near paralysis of royal attempts to reform the lower courts. Like royal efforts to reform so many other French institutions in the eighteenth century before the Revolution, the attempts were hamstrung by the failure either to resolve or to choose between traditional and modern reform and their different objectives.

The dialogue during the eighteenth century on reforming the lower courts, as it is revealed in the memorials sent to the crown and in other documents and treatises, focused on the présidiaux. The reasons for concentrating on the présidiaux had to do, on the one hand, with the peculiarly depressed condition of these courts due to the inadequate arrangements made for them and, on the other hand, with the modern characteristics that these courts seemed ideally to have. A political motive also led the crown to look at the présidiaux, for it saw in them—if they could be considerably upgraded—a possible tool to use against the parlements.

"Let us not search afar that which we have near at hand," said the winner of an essay competition sponsored by the Academy of Châlons-sur-Marne in 1782 on the question, "What would be the means of rendering justice in France with the most celerity and the least cost possible?" "Let us know to enjoy our advantages. The présidialité is a means as sure as it is simple and easy of shortening trials and diminishing fees. As all of France expresses itself in one voice for this abbreviation, this diminution, it also speaks in one voice for the présidialité. Every time one complains of the abuse, one shows at once the remedy: it is the présidial."[4] The essayist was himself, it must be noted, procureur du roi at the Présidial of Beauvais. It may also be assumed that the members of the Châlons academy who awarded the prize to him had an interest in the présidiaux because of the importance of their own présidial. But the concern with these courts was, as the prize essayist of 1782 stated, more general, and it had been deepened in the eighteenth century by Chancellor d'Aguesseau, the keeper of the seals Lamoignon de Basville, and other royal officials who had no personal interest in these courts.

## A Judiciary Aggrieved

### The Frustration of New Aspirations

What is most tantalizing about the memorials that the lower courts submitted to the crown in the eighteenth century is the evidence that they occasionally give of a developing consensus of the crown and the judiciary on reform, a consensus that a wise, perceptive monarch might have seen and nurtured, but which was missed and allowed to die. In their petitions for restoring the courts some of the judges came very close to the most extreme royal designs. If no court, for instance, wanted to be itself the object of a program of consolidation, many judges agreed, at least in principle, with the consolidation of jurisdictions. Members of the Bailliage of Châteaulin in Brittany, for example, urged the crown "to reduce jurisdictions to two levels—the lower, for handling the preliminary exami-

nation and judging provisionally the matters that are submitted to
it, and the sovereign, for deciding the good or bad judged by the first
judges—instead of the four or five degrees of jurisdiction that one
often has to face before obtaining a final judgment."[5] Some judges
also seemed to yearn for the higher standards that d'Aguesseau had
believed to be so important. One went so far, indeed, as to suggest
that he favored not just limitations on the sale of offices but the end
of it, and to call not just for a reduction in the fees collected by
judges but for their elimination. "There is no reasonable man,"
wrote this judge, in submitting a plan for rendering justice free of
charge, "who is not inwardly revolted by the venality of offices and
of Justice."[6]

The memorials sent in by the courts have been largely dismissed
by historians—as they were also by the crown, despite its object in
soliciting them—as petitions for personal privileges, jurisdictional
advantages over rival courts, and greater opportunities for income.
Often singled out for special criticism is the demand of judges in
présidial courts to be elevated to nobility. Vanity and desire for tax
exemptions may not have motivated this demand so much, however,
as the growing concern of judges that without nobility more and
more avenues of professional advancement and upward mobility
would be closed to them and, more importantly, to their children.
This concern was voiced quite openly and given as the principal
reason for their demanding noble status by the members of one
présidial in 1782. "Several parlements," they noted,

among others that of Toulouse, anxious to preserve the honor and the dignity of
their bodies, have made a solemn resolution to admit to themselves only nobles.
His majesty has also closed to the children of the présidial officers entrance to the
military profession by his last ordonnance, which required four degrees of nobility in the aspirants to this profession. It is not then possible that these magistrates
be deprived any longer of a favor that is becoming absolutely necessary to restore
the dignity of their positions and to procure for their children opportunities analogous to the sentiments of honor that they have received from their fathers.[7]

By demanding nobility, judges were making a legitimate request
for the guarantee of opportunities for promotion. The demand was
consistent with other of the judges' demands, such as those for
higher and more regularly paid gages, the renovation of dilapidated
*palais de justice,* and the limitation of *attributions* and other incursions
by the parlements on their jurisdictions. Behind all of the demands

was the idea that for professional work one deserves professional treatment. The uncertain and unregulated rewards obtainable by judges under the venal regime as it had operated since the sixteenth century were no longer acceptable. In part this was so because those rewards were no longer very great relative to those available elsewhere. But it was also because of a sharper sense of professionalism among judges, entailing a desire for fixed, rationally determined salaries and other benefits corresponding to one's position in a professional hierarchy. It was a professionalism that the crown might have exploited, but which it instead overlooked as it read the judges' petitions literally and responded to them accordingly.

### The Grinding of Salt into Long-Open Wounds

By the judges' estimations, the decline in income from their offices was not only relative to what equivalent investments in commerce or in some other offices in the royal administration would have earned, but was also absolute. Before the reign of Louis XIV, in the judges' view, their offices had been worth more. Lower court judges claimed, in fact, that they were showing annual net losses, and they complained of considerable diminution in the value of their offices. Members of the Sénéchaussée of Guérande spoke of a 45–60% decline in the sale prices of their offices between 1690 and 1735 over the prices that the offices had fetched before 1667.[8] "So many disastrous occurrences, so many revolutions so strange have so changed and disfigured [our seat]," wrote the Présidial of Nantes, "that it is today no more than the shadow of what it was in former times, and it sees its ruin near and inevitable."[9] It was absolutely essential, stated the Présidial of Vannes, that "things be reestablished to the state in which they were before the last wars."[10]

The judges of the Sénéchaussée of Ploermel described a reduction of two-thirds in both the revenues and prices of their offices. They said that their loss was compounded by the maintenance of the *prêt* (an obligatory and nonrepayable "loan" made to the crown by officeholders every nine years) and the *annuel* (an annual tax paid to the crown by officeholders to insure the heritability of their offices) at their same "exorbitant" levels and by the failure of the crown to increase gages despite an inflation of 50% (over what period of time, the judges did not specify) that had "reduced [the gages] to sums very little proportionate to [the judges'] labor."[11]

In a group-written memorial that they submitted to the crown in 1772, the sénéchaussées of Béarn asserted that their gages had actually been reduced, from 135 to 60 livres. At 60 livres, the judges claimed that the gages did not even suffice to pay the prêt and the annuel, which they still owed, they said, "although [we] paid to extinguish them a considerable amount, which [we] have not been reimbursed." (In 1709, Louis XIV had tried, generally with little success except in the case of Béarn, to get officeholders to redeem the prêt and the annuel.) The Béarn judges reinforced their assertion that their gages were effectively "reduced to nothing" by reporting their increased "upkeep expenses, be they for clothing, be they for *la vie animale.*" They cited an author named Dulot who had "demonstrated in his treatise on the revolution of monies that commodities are fifteen times dearer than in the sixteenth century."[12] (The Présidial of Nantes told of a more modest, 300% inflation since the 1550s.)[13]

To the judges, the most maddening of the financial expedients adopted by the crown at their expense was the creation of new offices that the judges were obliged to buy. The Sénéchaussée of Guérande recited a long list of offices created by Louis XIV in particular that were either combined with its jurisdiction or given functions so central to justice that it could not very well allow the offices to be purchased and exercised by any other body. Droits of the new offices were often not paid, and the officers' resulting requests for reimbursement of the sums that they may have gone into considerable debt to raise to buy the offices were seldom heeded. The judges of Guérande claimed that the gages for an office of *lieutenant général de police* created in their ressort in 1705 and purchased by them in the same year were thirty-three years in arrears.[14]

Members of the Présidial of Nantes told of a case in which they had been obliged to purchase three sets of offices. Having owned the two local offices of *enquêteur* ("investigating commissioner") since the 1570s, the présidial judges first saw the king separate from those offices the functions of *taxateurs de dépens* (to be responsible for fixing the legal costs of suits judged in the court) in 1689. In 1693 a new edict suppressed some of the remaining functions of the enquêteurs (including the making of investigations, the placing and breaking of the seal, the certification of acknowledgments of indebtedness and absence of indebtedness, and attendance at inventories of property), attributed them to four *commissaires enquêteurs,* and said that anyone who had the money was eligible to buy the new positions. The judges had no sooner arranged for the financing to rejoin these essential functions of the enquêteurs to their company when, in 1702, another edict of Louis XIV again detached some of the functions, attributing them this time to *commissaires aux inventaires.* "An event so extraordinary," wrote the judges, "and so little expected consternated more than ever the officers of the Présidial of Nantes: their credit was fallen, however they made a new effort, in the hope of not losing what had cost them so much money."[15]

Judges could not always, of course, afford to buy the new offices, and in cases where they could not, depending on who took over the former functions of the judges, the results could be detrimental or even chaotic for the administration of justice in a particular locale. The judges of Nantes, for instance, were not so successful with respect to preserving other functions of the enquêteurs. Also in 1689, the crown had separated the functions of setting the salaries and *vacations* of the procureurs of the seat from the offices of the enquêteurs and reassigned them to three *référendaires* ("chief clerks"), which it put on sale. The procureurs of Nantes, "always attentive and zealous for their interests," in the words of the judges, "did not let escape such a handsome opportunity to serve them and resolved to unite the offices to their *communauté."* The présidial could not outbid the procureurs, and the latter "thus became the masters and the sole arbiters of their salary and vacation, in straight defiance of subordination."[16]

The judges retired, as they had to, a great many offices in the late seventeenth and early eighteenth century. The need to service the mounting debts that they thus incurred was an important part of the financial unattractiveness of their positions during the remainder of the Old Regime. That only eight of twenty-eight offices in their seat were filled in 1766, the members of the Présidial of Limoux ascribed to the debts of their company, a portion of which new officers would have been expected to assume.[17] Of the 31,155 livres owed by the company in 1766, 13,905, or 45%, had been borrowed (between 1694 and 1705) to pay the cost of *augmentations des gages,* another financial expedient of the crown granted, or imposed, in return for officers' advancing more *finances* to the crown. 4000 livres, or 13%, went to pay the finances of some commissaires des inventaires in 1703 and of a *lieutenant général d'épée* that was joined to the company in 1706; and the rest went mainly to refinance earlier loans.[18]

### Other Actions of the Crown Bewildering to the Judges, and Shifts in the Economic Macrocosm

Another aspect of the financial unattractiveness of judgeships in the lower courts was the progressive loss of cases by those courts. The reasons for the loss of cases were several. First of all, the limits on the size of civil suits that the lower courts could try had not been raised since the sixteenth century in spite of the tremendous inflation that had occurred. This was at all times a principal grievance of judges in the présidiaux. Second, many exceptional jurisdictions, such as the *amirautés* and the *généraux provinciaux des monnaies* (the establishment of one of which in 1696 the Présidial of Nantes said had "despoiled" it of cognizance over counterfeiting cases),[19] had been set up. By the description of the courts in one province, the exceptional jurisdictions had reduced the ordinary courts "to limits so narrow that the consideration and respect due to the ancient luster and authority of the courts has turned nearly to contempt and the courts have been left in a sort of degradation."[20] Finally, the lesser royal jurisdictions had been further "dismembered" by the raising of seignorial jurisdictions in their midst.

Even as the crown had sought to extend its justice, it had shown, by enhancing old or setting up new seignorial courts, how habituated it was to working at cross-purposes. The Présidial of Nantes claimed to be "perhaps the company of the realm that has suffered the most from these dismemberments of functions." It told how, when the barony of Retz was elevated to a ducal peerage in 1581, it had lost fully one-fifth of its ressort, appeals from the seignorial court of Retz thenceforth being taken straight to the Parlement of Brittany. When the Isle of Boüin became a barony in 1713 and was wholly joined to the province of Poitou, the Présidial of Nantes lost another part of its ressort, appeals by those living in that part of the island seigniory formerly regarded as part of Brittany now going elsewhere.[21]

When the duchy of Joyeuse was erected in 1581 for one of the favorites of Henry III, the Présidial of Nîmes continued to take de facto cognizance over appeals made by the inhabitants of that district of its ressort and also continued to judge in the first instance the cases of noblemen who lived there. In the early 1700s, however, arrangements were made for the duchy finally to take over all the cases to which it was entitled and to allow its inhabitants to take their cases on appeal right to the parlement rather than to the présidial. The judges of the présidial were to be indemnified for their loss, but they did not regard the indemnification as adequate.[22]

While these situations were fairly clear-cut, in other situations the matter of where cases were to go was more confused. Many people apparently took their cases on appeal from both exceptional and seignorial courts—and some noblemen took their cases in the first instance—directly to the parlements even when their cases seemed to fall within the appellate or original jurisdiction of the présidiaux. D'Aguesseau wrote to the Intendant of Franche-Comté in June 1740, begging him to suggest the cure for a forty-year-old complaint of the Présidial of Vesoul that the noblemen living in the ressort of the présidial customarily took présidial cases straight to the parlement.[23]

The combined effect of the declining value of the judges' gages, the debts that judges had to contract to counter the financial tricks of the crown, and the continual raiding of the judges' jurisdictions by both higher and lower courts was devastating to the financial attractiveness of lower-court offices. But two other events further depressed the prices of judicial offices. Greater opportunities for investment opened up in industry and commerce. And professional expectations formed that were not to be met by court offices.

The implications of the growth of business for the market in offices are evident from some of the judges' memorials. Rather than subjecting themselves to the exploitative policies of the crown toward venal officeholders, people with ambition and the money required to purchase an office could do something else. In Languedoc, delegates of the provincial estates noted with concern that the présidiaux were "threatened with a complete desertion."[24] The officers of the Présidial of Béziers commented on the reasons for unfilled seats at two neighboring présidiaux. In Carcassonne, "cloth factories obtain the preference and reward labor with the solid advantages of fortune." In Montpellier, the competition for investor interest was even stiffer:

The city of Montpellier, which contains great fortunes and in quantity, not only offers to its citizens who have acquired them places more elevated in the magistrature [in the Bureau des finances and the Cour des comptes, aides, et finances of that city], perhaps less difficult and of a revenue more assured than the offices and especially the inferior offices in its présidial, but also these superior places, many honorable and lucrative employments, a flourishing commerce, which are there the portion or the object of ambition of everyone, make regarded at least with indifference the courts below the présidial, which find themselves extremely eclipsed.[25]

In the view of the Présidial of Limoux, the very "génie," or character, of the inhabitants of Carcassonne, now led them to favor trade over judicial offices:

The taste for commerce dominates in this city over all other tastes, and nothing is more opposed to the spirit of the magistrature than that of commerce. How could the son of a magistrate, surrounded by young men of his age raised for commerce, resist the impressions that must be made on a young heart by the comparison of these two states? He will see the sons of the négociants swimming in opulence and satisfying all their wishes. How could he prefer the quiet virtues and the happy mediocrity that go with the magistrature to the glitter of luxury and ease? The lessons that he will receive at home, will they hold their own against the more seductive lessons that will be taught to him away from home by his companions?[26]

While in the sixteenth century, L'Hospital had been able to state with assurance that "no source of gain and return is more certain . . . than that of offices," by the eighteenth century the consensus of opinion on this point had changed.

Looking back on the eighteenth century, one may see that the sudden attractiveness of trade resulted from broad global developments. The judges, however, returned again and again to the policies of the crown. As long as the crown had preserved the functions of the courts intact, said the Présidial of Nantes, the moderate gages had been reasonable. For the cases coming into the courts had sufficed to produce "a revenue well enough proportioned to the sums that one had employed to acquire [the court offices]." "But barely had one seen," the judges continued, "formed from the remains of those functions entire seats and companies of justice not indemnified [for the full jurisdictions that were not given to them] than the public ceased to give its esteem and carry its ambition to [the profession of justice]. So it was that an infinity of men of merit who had all the qualities necessary for the magistrature and who had regarded these offices as places of honor and distinction despised them and made their careers elsewhere."[27]

New professional expectations heightened dissatisfaction with the judicial occupation. "Reason," wrote a judge of the Présidial of Limoux, "is it not shocked at seeing that a *conseiller* in the présidial has only 50 livres in gages, which one would not dare to offer today to the lowest lackey?" Men starting their careers, according to this judge, were more often choosing positions where the pay corresponded to the dignity and importance of the responsibilities. "A young avocat of this city," he said,

gifted with all the qualities required for a magistrate, refused to raise an office in the présidial from the parties casuelles and preferred to acquire for a sum of 3000 livres the offices of *contrôleur des tailles* in the same city fallen to the parties casuelles because they give him around 1000 livres of revenue. Another young avocat, gifted with the same qualities, actually pursues the temporary allowance of *notaire* because he hopes to join with it the *commission du contrôle*, which yields 800–900 livres.[28]

Some lawyers may, for the same reasons, have been choosing to continue practicing law instead of going into the judiciary. One notes a letter in 1740 from an avocat in Auvergne to the intendant of his province, "announcing that, his poor health obliging him to renounce his profession of avocat, he had purchased a position as conseiller in the Présidial [of Riom]."[29] The writer of the letter implied that had he still been vigorous he would have remained a lawyer.

The enactment in 1695 of the *capitation* ("head tax"), which assessed Frenchmen according to their title, position, or occupation, may have given an impetus to the movement away from offices in the lower royal courts, as Frenchmen sought offices or professions that actually yielded the income that the crown had implied they should. The principal officers of the provincial présidiaux found themselves grouped in the eleventh and twelfth classes (assessed, respectively, at 100 and 80 livres) with, among others, wholesale merchants and sellers of fresh seafish. Below them were nearly all (untitled and non-officeholding) men of business, both large and small, except bankers and stockbrokers (who were in the tenth class, assessed at 120 livres).[30]

Prior to the capitation, one might hypothesize, judicial officers were satisfied that the status they derived from their offices made up for what they lacked in income from them. Possibly those buying or inheriting présidial offices were also richer to start with in the earlier time. Pierre Goubert has said that in the seventeenth century, not only did the judges' offices generally constitute a "secondary and sometimes insignificant" portion of their total assets, but also that the revenues the officers earned formed only "a small part" of their total personal revenues.[31]

Regardless of their condition in earlier times, judges in the eighteenth century complained not only that their income was lacking but also that their status was becoming questionable. In the memorials that they addressed to the crown, numerous judges complained, for example, that they were sometimes being asked to shelter troops, an obligation from which they had formerly been specifically exempted by virtue of their positions. The judges of the Présidial of Nîmes wrote that they were apparently becoming "exposed to all the disagreeable things that afflict those who are not nobles," as evidenced by "an unjust decision that subjected a conseiller of the Présidial of Gray to furnish lodging to soldiers."[32] The Présidial of Quimper cited the "confounding of the conseillers of the présidial with the least inhabitants in imposing on them the barracking of militiamen and other vile subsidies."[33] The Présidial of Nantes gave a somewhat fuller list of the indignities and burdens to which its members were susceptible, demanding that the king:

accord to the officers of the présidiaux privileges that could distinguish them from the common people and take them from the midst of the basest populace, with which they find themselves confounded by the shameful contribution to the billeting of troops and militiamen and the responsibility for tutelage and guardianship that takes away from them part of the time and attention that they owe to their offices and the public; while at the same time they experience the chagrin and the confusion of seeing the least significant officers, down to the beadles of the universities [in the nineteenth class, assessed at six livres, for the capitation] and others, gratified with all sorts of privileges and prerogatives.[34]

As well as the restoration of their status, the judges demanded appropriate income. Without it, according to the judge from the Présidial of Limoux, "the seats will be deserted, because generosity and patriotism are rare. Profit alone attracts subjects because it procures the necessities of life."[35] But the judges' demand for more income was not due simply to their desire to make up for what they had lost through the effects of inflation, dismemberments of ressorts, reductions of gages, and the depredations of the crown. Rather, the requests of some judges for gages that would by themselves fully compensate them for their labor revealed a new, or at least different, sense of professionalism. Judges no longer wanted their compensation to be left to chance or their opportunities for promotion to be subject to diminution by the vagaries of social exclusion. Rather, they wanted both to be firmly established and clearly tied to the importance of the responsibilities they had assumed on taking their offices.

It was precisely this willingness of judges to surrender the unconditional authority the crown had given them when it had started selling offices in the sixteenth century and to take instead fixed salaries that had always been the missing condition for the success of professional and disciplinary reforms of the judiciary. Certainly not all and probably not even a majority of judges were willing by the eighteenth century to settle for salaries. But enough of them may have decided that only salaries could make their positions worthwhile that the crown might successfully have imposed at this time, or started gradually to introduce, some very significant changes in the way judges were paid. The crown itself had, by its actions during the latter part of the seventeenth and the early eighteenth centuries, most notably perhaps by its enactment of the capitation, helped create this condition for reform. No less unintentionally, the crown failed to take advantage of it during the remainder of the eighteenth century.

Another stumbling block to the establishment of professionalism in the judiciary had been the inability of the crown to find the money for it. With this problem, unfortunately, the judges' memorials did not give the crown much help. The one plan found among them for establishing la justice gratuite, that in 1766 of Maguelone de St. Benoit, the judge of the Présidial of Limoux, showed no improvement, at least with respect to feasibility, over the plans of L'Hospital and Du Noyer. But while Maguelone's proposal would surely not have worked any better than the proposals of his predecessors, it differed from theirs in showing characteristics of modern reform. Indeed it also manifested the confusion of traditional and modern reform typical of the judges' memorials as well as of the programs of the crown.

### Blurred Views of Modern Solutions

The plan of Maguelone was to establish la justice gratuite "without its costing anything to the king or the state." This was to be accomplished by the crown's simply transferring to each city of France the fonds out of which it was currently paying the gages of the judges in that city, along with what Maguelone reckoned would have been a more sizable amount, a sum representing the value of all the judicial *charges* of the city fallen vacant to the parties casuelles. The cities would use the money thus turned over to them to set up their own fonds, out of which they would be able to pay judges much increased gages.

Of course Maguelone was asking the king to deliver what he almost certainly did not have, and far from costing the king nothing, this plan would have cost him a great deal. To think that the crown would still have the money paid in the sixteenth century for an office that had reverted to the crown in 1700—and that it would also have kept all of the various finances advanced to it by the different holders of the office along the way—was very fanciful. Perhaps Maguelone was not so naive as he appeared to be and intended his proposal mainly to embarrass the crown. Many other judges asked why, when there were fewer judges, the crown could not pay them more by distributing among them what it had been paying to holders of the judgeships that were vacant. The crown, it was true, had laid down many conditions for officeholders to meet unless they would forfeit their principal, but it had done this after borrowing the principal. For the crown to preserve some semblance of fairness it should continue at least to pay some interest on the loans that it would now never have to repay. And why not pay it to the remaining judges? Thus Maguelone's proposal may really have been designed to show how much the crown was making, or not paying in interest, on the debts that it had managed to elude.

Maguelone desired that judges' gages be raised sufficiently to fully compensate the magistrates for their work. In two detailed tables, he showed how, in the case of his own court at Limoux, a modest 5% return on the new fonds that he advocated would permit the payment of gages considerably higher than the total income that judges were then realizing from gages and épices.[36] (One is somewhat astonished to learn that Maguelone and the other judges of this présidial were already making annually nearly 7% on the purchase price of their offices; the augmented gages that Maguelone proposed would have given them an 11% return!) Each judge would then be able to have "an honest income" and "to do without odious épices and render justice free of charge." Unlike L'Hospital and Du Noyer—but like Saint-Pierre—Maguelone set down all of his calculations so that one could see exactly where the money would come from for each part of the program. 49,050 livres constituted the fonds from which the king was paying the gages of the judges of Limoux; the prices of all the vacant charges totaled 139,100 livres. The two sources together would yield a fonds of 188,150 livres for remunerating the judges.

Also like Saint-Pierre, he showed the logical consequences of the change that he urged. Not only would a typical judge earn more under Maguelone's system, but "he would [also] gain . . . tranquility of conscience; and, the law and its interpreters becoming more respected by the people, there would be fewer crimes."[37] His confidence in the plan—indeed his impatience with those who would not implement it—was yet a third manifestation of the modern influence that was at work on Maguelone.

While the plan of the judge from Limoux had modern characteristics, it would have stopped far short of completely restructuring the judiciary. Furthermore, the structural reform that it did comprise—putting the judges on strict salaries—probably would not have succeeded in its aims unless the other long-advocated, major structural reform—ending the ownership of judicial offices—had also been achieved. Maguelone seemingly contradicted himself on the subject of the venality of offices. Although he spoke of one's "inward revulsion" at the sale of offices, he would have done nothing to end it. Instead, in another document, he justified the venal regime with the customary arguments that it insured a more qualified and less corruptible judiciary than some other system of recruitment might have supplied.[38] For it insured that the rich and not the poor would be judges. Education, he said, contributes more to "the morals, capacity, and sentiments" than "nature." "The rich," he continued, "commonly spare nothing for the education of their children; the poor cannot furnish it." Extending the other prong of his argument, he concluded thus, "It is then more advantageous to the public to have magistrates rather rich than poor. Necessity, need often make the poor magistrate forget the dignity of his position, and there are only too many examples that make the voices of companies groan over the members that dishonor them."

But without the abolition of the sale of offices, judges like Maguelone who were disgusted by it would not, first of all, have experienced fully that "tranquility of conscience" that was one aim of the plan. Second, by having, theoretically, paid all of the money that was to have gone into the new fonds, the judges would still have been receiving income on their own investments rather than salaries in the strict sense. However the judges may have yearned for professional status, they would thus still have been subject, under Maguelone's plan, to the propensity to maximize the return on their investments. Maguelone's detailing of the finances required to produce an 11% income for the judges of his seat may indicate how large the minimum return was that judges considered reasonable. If the whole fonds could not have been put together, which would seem to have been a more than likely possibility, the tendency would have existed for judges to make up in other ways the rest of the income to which they felt entitled. Third, the people would still have perceived that judges held their positions primarily because of their wealth and may consequently not have accorded the judges, and the whole system of justice, the increased respect that Maguelone said would lead to a decrease in crime.

While Maguelone's plan called, then, for new compensation for judges, it did not outline a new source for that compensation. On the contrary, at every point in his presentation, Maguelone hastened to show that the public would not have to pay more taxes, that the public, in essence, would no longer have to pay in any way for justice. During the Revolution it would be seen that to achieve a judiciary responsible to the public, the public should be made responsible for the judiciary. Indeed, since the revolutionaries regarded justice as an attribute of the popular sovereignty rather than of the king, they could hardly have had it otherwise.

Maguelone seemed uncertain whether justice was the king's or the people's, which was perhaps an important reason for the shortcomings in his plan. He wanted judges to be able to respect themselves, to know from the compensation they received that they were doing something useful. He did not take the next step, however, and say that the only way for judges to know for sure that they were being useful, whether to the king or to the people, was to be compensated by those to whom they were of use—not in the customary manner of being paid interest on their capital investments, or épices that they more or less regulated themselves, but by being apportioned a share of the state revenue. Instead he left his plan in confusion. He equated his traditional proposal to tap fully the supposedly existing sources of funds, as in his view they were originally intended to be used, in order to pay judges higher gages with the modern reform of completely professionalizing the judiciary, which would in fact have entailed tearing up both the key structural foundations of the French judiciary.

In the memorials submitted by other seats, one finds the recommendation to preserve and strengthen the courts by changing them internally. In the memoir of the Présidial of Béziers, for instance, was the statement:

one cannot conceal the fact that the . . . general reestablishment of the sénéchaussées . . . would be insufficient, and its efficacy would be of only little duration, because the decay of the sénéchaussées comes from the very form of their establishment. Before long, this cause of decay would make itself felt again if one did not substitute a new arrangement for the old to terminate forever the abuses and disorder inherent in it, which would be the perpetual cause of the decline of the sénéchaussées.[39]

And in an anonymous memorial, also from Languedoc, one sees expressed very similarly the idea that institutions should be regenerated from within:

The indispensable necessity of reestablishing the seats in question is generally recognized, but among the different means indicated, or even demanded, by all the companies . . . the best has perhaps been omitted. None of the courts has so far gone to the cause of the trouble, which is the very way in which the courts are constituted. All have demanded instead only palliative remedies, as it were, such that after an apparent return of vigor to the courts they would not be impeded from falling again very soon into the same decadence in which one sees them today.[40]

The memorials differed in some of the measures that they went on to suggest, but they both proposed clarifying and enhancing the role of the chief judge, the *juge mage*, of the présidiaux to give the courts more effective leadership and make them more efficient in their disposition of cases. "The first roots of reason and nature," stated the second memorial, "grow up gradually into the differences between all people, so that the order and harmony of the various parts of a company, and of a company of justice above all, have need essentially of a head capable of arranging all in the company, without which the company is allowed to corrupt itself by personal interest." For, the proposal argued, the présidiaux would not be able to secure more cases to try, no matter how many more potential cases they were offered by the crown, if their internal procedures were not improved to encourage people to bring their cases into them.

With all the courts surviving even after phasing out the lowest royal jurisdictions, the competition for cases among the courts in Old Regime France was very keen. Civil litigants in most areas had several different kinds of courts from which to choose. Hence the second memorial began by saying that the key to all successful reform of the présidiaux was to "balance at each step the public interest and the particular interest . . . of those employed to render justice." The reasoning was unobjectionable as far as it went, but like Maguelone's it did not address all the issues involved, let alone tackle the problem of either solidly bridging or completely separating traditional and modern reform. Despite their claim to be approaching the source of difficulty, the writers of neither memorial even touched, for instance, on the venality of judicial offices. They did not consider, as d'Aguesseau had, that the only way to achieve the kinds of results they hoped for from the holder of a chief judgeship such as they described was to make that position strictly appointive.

The memorials often overlapped the thinking of the crown to a remarkable extent. If the judges sometimes had different interests in mind than did the crown, they were frequently led to the same conclusions about the necessity of certain specific reforms. Moreover, the judges encountered the same difficulties as the crown in formulating means consistent with the ends they sought. Their memorials were as much a farrago of traditional and modern elements, approaches, and language as d'Aguesseau's, and seemingly as little conscious of the fact. As such, they must only have compounded the confusion about reform that the crown was already experiencing during this century.

That the lower courts were in a bad way, everyone agreed. The situation described for the new chancellor, Lamoignon de Blancmesnil, by the members of the Présidial of Cahors was not, all recognized, unique to Quercy. After reviewing the richer ressorts of some of their neighboring courts, the few remaining judges of Cahors sent up a cry of despair. "As we cannot doubt, Monseigneur, that despite the advantages that the [other] seats [of our country] enjoy over ours, their offices are equally fallen into discredit, we have grounds to fear that if ours remains as it is, it will be very soon entirely deserted. Its decadence becomes every day so tangible that the officeholders no longer regard the charges with which they are invested as objects worthwhile preserving in their families even though they represent to them a considerable part of their patrimony."[41]

The ramifications of the decay of the lower judiciary were also very worrisome. The Sénéchaussée of Lannion in Brittany was by no means alone in linking "the disgust for the office of judge and procureur du roi" with "the impunity of several crimes, or, in all cases, an extraordinary slowness in taking action against them, from which can only result great evils."[42] The Intendant of Languedoc wrote the chancellor of the dire state of affairs in his province in 1755:

For a very long time the majority of the ordinary royal seats in the province of Languedoc have been in the saddest condition owing to the lack of officers. Justice is not administered at all in the présidiaux, neither in civil nor in criminal matters; the prisoners languish in the jails or succeed in escaping from them; crime remains unpunished; the number of wrongdoers increases everywhere; the auxiliaries of justice are of such insolence that they declare the law to the judges; and the people bear the burden of a disorder that has need of a prompt and violent remedy to be corrected.[43]

What was at issue was how to mend the lower courts. Toward solving that problem, unfortunately, the memorials of the judges did not give the crown much help, or at least help that it was able to recognize.

### The Response of the Crown

"One left them in the same state," said the lawyer Linguet in 1764, referring to the failure of the crown to arrest the decline of the présidiaux over the preceding two centuries, "because one shrank from the effort necessary to introduce in them a useful change."[44] From what the crown had most shrunk, in the view of Linguet, was the task of protecting the présidiaux from the "jealousy" of the parlements. The parlements had regarded as an "affront," since the very creation of the présidiaux, all the efforts that the présidiaux had made to estab-

lish themselves in the judicial hierarchy. "Each time that the présidiaux made any effort to escape from the deadly torpor in which they
sensed themselves fallen," said Linguet, "the sovereign courts took a
delight in plunging them back into it." The crown had also shrunk,
he said, from suppressing the seignorial courts: "[The présidiaux]
were trees intended to be . . . the consolation and the ornament of the
provinces. But, unhappily, one planted them in ground covered with
brambles and undergrowth."[45]

The crown had likewise failed to adjust the jurisdictional limits of
the présidiaux to take into account what Linguet said had been
nearly a 345% inflation since the middle of the sixteenth century.
This inflation had resulted in the "engorgement" of the parlements
with cases and the contraction of the présidiaux. Finally, the crown
had failed to accord to présidial officers privileges and exemptions
comparable to those of officers in the higher courts. "The nudity of
one part," he said, "becomes more shocking by the adornment of the
other."[46] But the main shortcoming in the course that the crown had
followed in managing its judiciary was, Linguet asserted, the failure
to keep the parlements within their proper bounds. In repeating what
many of the présidial judges themselves had stated in their memorials, Linguet broadcast the rarely expressed idea that successful judicial reform in France would necessarily encompass the parlements,
too; that, in fact, restraints on the parlements were, if not the key, the
first prerequisite for effective change.

The crown had not established that prerequisite by the 1760s, as
Linguet noted—nor indeed, one could argue, by the 1780s—nor had
it even seriously tried to do so. What the crown did do for the lower
courts probably saved them from disappearing completely and even
from declining much further, but could hardly have made them any
more profitable for their members or effective as institutions of justice. In the eighteenth century, the crown did accelerate the process
that it had begun in the sixteenth century of phasing out the lowest
royal jurisdictions—those of the prévôts, vicomtes, châtelains, and
viguiers. The general suppression in 1749 of these jurisdictions in
places where there were also bailliages or sénéchaussées was, in fact,
the one real result of d'Aguesseau's program for strengthening the
latter courts.[47]

It is unlikely that this suppression helped the bailliages and
sénéchaussées very much. The prévôts and their equivalents had

had but one of a host of minor jurisdictions in most areas, and the other jurisdictions, including those of the *consuls des communautés,* the seigniors, and many others, remained. The only boon that the members of the Présidial of Béziers anticipated from the suppression of the viguerie in their city was the addition—promised by the edict of suppression—of the gages of the officers of that court to their own gages. But four years after the suppression they had yet to receive any of those gages.[48] The addition of the minor jurisdictions to their ressorts had only the effects of convincing the judges of the bailliages and sénéchaussées that the crown was not completely neglecting them and perhaps also of creating in their minds the expectation of further *réunions* in the future.

In the wake of the Maupeou years, the crown belatedly experimented with raising the jurisdictional limits of the présidiaux. Meeting opposition from the parlements, and also from the bailliages without présidial competence, the crown backed away. As with the réunion of the minor royal jurisdictions to the bailliages and sénéchaussées, the final result of the experiment of 1774–1778 could at best have encouraged the members of the présidiaux but certainly not have satisfied them.[49] With respect to the demand of the présidial officers for nobility, only the officers of the Châtelet became recipients, in 1768, of the prized status. Toward the officers of the présidiaux, the crown continued to exercise a parsimony with noble status that characterized its policy toward officeholders throughout the Old Regime. Only a tiny percentage of offices carried noble status, though many offices apparently carried financial advantages similar to those of nobles.

In the eighteenth century, opportunities for promotion to some of the highest offices were increasingly being closed to all but nobles, hence the lack of nobility was becoming more vexing. The crown's granting of nobility to the members of the Châtelet did not help the judges in the other présidiaux. It kept them, again, on a leash of expectations, but the leash chafed as they felt the crown drawing it in. More grounds for the officeholders' expectations needed to be established if the lower courts were to be strengthened rather than simply maintained in their same sorry state.

Meeting the requirements of judicial reform was a recurring concern of the French crown from the 1730s on. But when this concern came to the fore—as during d'Aguesseau's last term as keeper of the

seals (1737–1750), during the brief tenure of Feydeau de Brou as
keeper of the seals (1762–1763), and during the late 1760s, early and
middle 1770s, and late 1780s, when Maupeou (the younger), Miromesnil, and Lamoignon de Basville, in succession, had the seals[50]—
either the crown attached to it a low priority or was prompted to
act only by other problems whose solutions were in certain ways dependent on reforming the courts. Only the period from 1750–1762
would seem to have been a hiatus in the post–1730 history of the attempts of the crown at court reform. The controversy with the Parlement of Paris over the sacraments claimed the attention of the
chancellor, Lamoignon de Blancmesnil, during the first half of the
1750s;[51] taxation, then the navy, were the predominant concerns of
Machault, who always united the seals with another office. One has
only to look at the names of the last two keepers of the seals during
this period—Louis XV and Berryer—and to remember that the
most costly and disastrous of all the wars of the reign of Louis XV,
the Seven Years War, had started in 1756 to realize that judicial reform could not have been a very great concern of the crown in the
years 1757–1762. But even at the high-water marks in the history of
its attempts at court reform, the crown's actions left much to be desired.

Why did the crown do so little, especially when the memorials
from the lower courts would seem to have confirmed the worst anxieties that the crown had expressed when it solicited them? A breakdown of justice and resulting disorder cannot have been an occurrence that the crown would have viewed with equanimity. Several
reasons may be suggested for the crown's not having done more. The
lower courts, first of all, were not all on the verge of collapse; some, in
fact, were flourishing.[52] Most of the memorials quoted here were from
courts in Brittany and Languedoc, poorer and also more poorly
governed areas, where one would have expected to find both the
lower courts and the system of justice in general in worse condition
than elsewhere.

Second, a court's relative prosperity or misery was related closely
to the relative strength or weakness of the economic life of the area in
which it was situated. Thus the crown, short of moving courts or completely professionalizing the judiciary, may not have been able to do
much for many of the courts. The Présidial of Tours, for example,
found itself rather haplessly situated in a city declining both eco-

nomically and demographically in the eighteenth century. Even so, however—and this leads to a third point—the lack of *audiences* ("sessions") in the Présidial of Tours, when it occurred, was apparently due to personal feuding between the judges of the seat as much as to a shortage of judges.[53] For that and similar reasons, the crown may very properly have been skeptical of many of the memorials of lower-court judges protesting their inability to perform their functions. And fourth, the close supervision of justice by the intendants over the course of the seventeenth and eighteenth centuries had probably eliminated some of the opportunities for making extra money that may have helped attract people to judicial offices in earlier times. Hence some of the judges' demands that the crown provide them with more income might justifiably have been dismissed as disingenuous.

None of these reasons would, however, completely justify the crown's inaction. Though the state of the courts of law and justice in general in Brittany and Languedoc was surely worse than that which obtained elsewhere, it was probably but a more extreme case of the malady that one found in many of those other places as well. Second, the strength of local economies often depended just as much on the vitality of the local courts as the courts did on the local economies, judicial officers both attracting and themselves accounting for a very large portion of the market for goods and services in their community. Third, there was much agreement among the authors of the memorials on the essential reasons for the decline of the lower courts. Intracompany feuding like that contributing to the occasional inactivity of the Présidial of Tours was surely not the explanation everywhere of the courts' decay. Finally, only the most extortionist fiscal policies of the crown toward its officeholders could have accounted for the most severe decline in the returns that judges realized from their positions.

The actual thoughts of the crown upon receiving the memorials from the lower courts are, for the most part, not recorded. Thus the reasons for its doing so little to assuage the plight of those courts can only be conjectured. It seems likely, though, that the response of the crown was so often negative not because the memorials failed to convince the crown that the needs of the lower courts were urgent, but because the crown was confused about its aims with respect to the lower courts and the memorials did nothing but compound that confusion. An illuminating exchange in this regard is one between the chancellor, Lamoignon de Blancmesnil, and the Intendant of Languedoc, Guignard de Saint-Priest, in the early 1750s. (Before he was totally distracted by the controversy over the sacraments, Lamoignon, following in the steps of d'Aguesseau, requested memoirs on the state of the lower courts from the intendants. Although he was unable to act on any of them, he did evidently comment on them and devote some of his own thoughts to possible solutions of the problems that the memoirs described.)

In reply to a letter from the chancellor in 1752, the intendant submitted a memorial that he had secured from the Présidial of Montpellier and added to it some of his personal ideas. To insure an adequate number of judges to hold audiences, the magistrates, he said, had proposed a number of measures, most notably the reestablishment of a Cour des monnaies in Montpellier (by carving out a portion of the "very extended" ressort of the Cour des monnaies of Lyon) and the union of it with the présidial. The intendant suggested that an easier and quicker way to give the présidial the judges that it needed would be to unite the law faculty of Montpellier, with its five professors and six *docteurs agrégés* (as well as its more spacious building), to the présidial.[54]

Lamoignon wrote back to Guignard the same year, stating that although such a change as the intendant proposed offered "a very great advantage in that it would immediately produce the number of judges necessary for the administration of justice," the functions of judges and law professors were "so little analogous" that "a great number of inconveniences" might arise from their merger. Without elaborating, he went on to share his own thoughts on the matter of reforming the présidial. One could insure the requisite number of judges still more economically, he said, by stipulating that some of the senior avocats of the seat would substitute for judges when needed and by requiring that no one could become a judge in the more prestigious Cour des comptes, aides, et finances of Montpellier without first serving in the présidial.

Going further, the chancellor proposed a comprehensive reform of all the royal courts in Languedoc that involved suppressing all the ordinary royal jurisdictions of the province (below the parlement) and "creating from them new ones" that would be divided into four classes. Instead of the seven présidiaux that Languedoc had, there would be only two, one at Nîmes and the other at Montpellier. Simple sénéchaussées, *sénéchaux,* and *sièges subalternes,* each with a uniform number of officers, would form the other three classes of royal courts. In addition, the chancellor announced his intention to exempt the judges from the *taille personnelle* (which Guignard observed would have been meaningless since the *taille* in Languedoc was *réelle*) and the *logement des gens de guerre* ("billeting of troops") and to accord gradual nobility to the chief judge of each présidial.[55]

The proposals of judges, intendant, and chancellor alike remained on paper. One can see, however, that the proposals were characterized by the typically baffling, eighteenth-century combination of traditional and modern reforms, which would have made them extremely difficult to enact. The judges proposed a more equitable division of ressorts and a novel consolidation of kinds of jurisdictions as the means to conserve existing courts. The chancellor proposed status-supportive reforms similar to those that the judges had demanded at the same time as he outlined a plan for reworking all the jurisdictions of Languedoc that would have upset the relative status of most of the judges. How, one might have asked the judges, could the ressort of the Cour des monnaies of Lyon have been reduced without that court's being weakened? Was it not inconsistent to propose a scheme for conserving existing courts that would only have placed some of them in greater need of conservation? How, one might have asked the chancellor, was bolstering the traditional status of the judges to have helped in the face of a nearly total upheaval of the institutional hierarchy that was the source of their status? Did the crown aim at restoring the old system of justice or creating a new one?

The evident confusion of the crown about its goals for the judiciary was most striking and consequential during the administration of Lamoignon's successor as chancellor, Maupeou the younger. But also in the period before Maupeou, the crown was taking new directions in court reform at the same time as it pursued old ones and was consequently making little progress in either direction. A member of the Présidial of Orléans, Guillaume-François Le Trosne, aptly summed up the danger that the crown was running by its inability to decide whether it would restore the présidiaux (and indeed the whole system of justice) or remake them—namely, that its continued inaction would soon leave it no choice. "If the re-establishment of the présidiaux is yet deferred a certain number of years," he said, "there will no longer be time to provide for it; their ruin will be consummated. It will be necessary to create new tribunals; and what difficulty will one not find in filling them, when the example for imitation, which leads the majority of men, will have wholly ceased to dazzle them; when deep prejudices will have turned away all the subjects from this profession and time will have fortified more and more that public opinion that from it turns."[56] The actions of the next chancellor would only increase the prejudices that Le Trosne noted against the Old Regime judiciary as a way of professional life.

# 4 / A Misfeatured Attempt at Reform and Its Aftermath

## A Perspective on Maupeou

"If God, from out of his divine whims, sent to earth an agent to reform our abuses, he would begin by doing what Louis XV is doing in this part of the administration." So spoke Voltaire in 1771 of the drastic changes that Louis XV was authorizing Chancellor Maupeou to make in the French judiciary during the last years of his reign.[1] Historians have long considered it a possibility, however, that Maupeou was rather caught by surprise at the resolute opposition he encountered even from the Grand'Chambre of the Parlement of Paris in late 1770 and early 1771, when he called the bluff of the parlement and found that it was not bluffing; that the subsequent reforms of the parlements were a strictly adventitious aspect of the reign of Louis XV.[2] The suggestions for reforming the parlements that his assistant Lebrun had earlier put forward, Maupeou may thus have considered only when his attempt to break the will of the parlements unexpectedly failed, justice ceased, and he really had no choice but to construct new courts.[3] It is likely, that is, that he did not set out to reform the parlements. The most recent scholarship has suggested, in fact, that Maupeou had probably intended to do nothing more ambitious than follow the lead of d'Aguesseau and Lamoignon de Blancmesnil and work on reforming the présidiaux and other lower courts.[4]

That Maupeou's changes in the parlements and establishment of *conseils supérieurs* within the ressorts of some of them were even accidental reforms was debatable in the eighteenth century. Linguet, as an attorney for the Duke d'Aiguillon, naturally started out as a supporter for Maupeou, but soon swung over to the opposition. In a later work, he compared the "transitory revolution of 1771" to the "reform of 1788." "This alleged revolution of 1771," he wrote, "in its origin, in its details, in its catastrophe, even in its annihilation, was truly only a ministerial quarrel, only a jealous dispute between ambitious rivals. The parlements, led themselves by another ambition, by another jealousy, after having been first the instruments, then the victims of the rivals, were the pretexts for a vengeance more artistically devised than one should have expected there."[5] One of the kings generally considered an enlightened monarch, who might have seen the Maupeou edicts as a kindred "reform from the top," did not consider the possibility that they were ever intended to be such. Writing to Marie Antoinette in May 1774, Joseph II summed up the last part of the reign of the late king. "The nation groaned under the burden which had been imposed upon them of late years by Louis XV. He dissolved the parliaments, gave his favorites too much power over the people, and removed the Choiseuls, Malesherbes, and the Chalotais. He placed at the helm of affairs men like Maupeou, the odious Abbé Terray, and the Duke d'Aiguillon, who, with the abominable Du Barry, plundered and distracted the kingdom; and this deprived him of the love of his people."[6]

Even if the self-justifying compte rendu that Maupeou sent to Louis XVI in 1789 is not to be regarded as the whole story, however, the edicts of Maupeou must still be admitted as reforms.[7] For change the judiciary they certainly did, and no matter what the motive behind them, they embodied several of the long-standing proposals for judicial reform that have been the subject of this discussion. To rub the Maupeou edicts against any more fastidious touchstone is unwarranted. One may also accept Maupeou as their author. The most cursory inspection, it is true, shows the close correspondence between much of the chancellor's compte rendu and the memoir that Lebrun wrote for the chancellor in 1769 (and also the speeches that Lebrun wrote for him in 1770–1771).[8] One must, however, accept the thoughts expressed in the compte rendu as the chancellor's own at least in the sense that he had put them forward and, however imperfectly, defended them.

The largely disastrous consequences of the Maupeou edicts may be seen to have been due not so much to an uneven quality in the reforms that they instituted—though that was undeniably a characteristic of them—as to a confusion of traditional and modern approaches in the reforms similar to that of royal reform throughout the century. It may be argued, in fact, that it was only the more pronounced confusion in Maupeou's program that made his reforms

appear so much more suspect than previous (and subsequent) reforms. Maupeou himself admitted that his reforms were the result
"of an unforeseen necessity."[9] When this necessity presented itself he
took all the ideas that were at hand for reforming the judiciary and,
not having the leisure or perhaps the inclination to rethink them,
simply did what he could with them.

The idea, first of all, for carving up the ressorts, especially of the
larger parlements, may be found expressed in Saint-Pierre's writings
of the 1730s. The abbé called for five additional parlements in the
ressort of the Parlement of Paris (at Le Mans, Tours, Poitiers,
Amiens, and Bourges), as well as for the reassignment of the Bour-
bonnais to the Parlement of Grenoble; for an additional parlement
in Normandy and one in Brittany; and for an unspecified number of
new parlements in Guyenne and Languedoc.[10] Maupeou, of course,
did not create new parlements, but conseils supérieurs; and the conseils supérieurs that he set up in the ressort of the Parlement of Paris
were placed differently than the new courts that Saint-Pierre would
have created. (Maupeou's were at Blois, Arras, Châlons-sur-Marne,
Clermont-Ferrand, Lyon, and Poitiers.) But there were about the
same number of new courts in Maupeou's program as there were in
Saint-Pierre's for the Paris ressort, and the chancellor also set up one
more supreme jurisdiction in Normandy and one in Languedoc. In
both plans, the effect was that the new ressorts of the high courts
would be roughly equal in area; it was the idea for a geometrical
reapportionment of ressorts that had been forming since the seventeenth century that Maupeou obviously took as his guide for re-
building the French courts.[11]

Furthermore, the idea of ending the venality of judicial offices
had been around practically from the very moment that the offices
had become venal. Making judgeships strictly appointive, salaried
positions had, since L'Hospital at least, been seen as the surest, and
indeed as an essential, way for the crown to regain control of its judiciary. Lebrun had lectured Maupeou in 1769 on the clear and
constant threat to the crown posed by "bodies that can regard
themselves as purchasers and proprietors of a portion of the royal
authority ... [that] can either choose their members or adopt only
those who suit them."[12] While the chancellor was, as he himself said,
"far from intending to make this change by a sudden and general

movement," he did follow his assistant's advice to the extent of abolishing the ownership of office in his remodeled parlements and in the new conseils supérieurs.[13]

Among the other ideas for court reform upon which Maupeou acted were those for stopping the collection of épices, reducing the number of officers, and eliminating *cours d'exception*. He instituted la justice gratuite in the parlements and conseils supérieurs (paying salaries by raising taxes); cut the number of judges in the high courts by about one-half; and eliminated a handful of the exceptional jurisdictions. To end the political pretensions of the parlements, Maupeou apparently would have replaced all the parlements with conseils supérieurs, which were not allowed the right of remonstrance, but here Louis XV drew the line. The king evidently thought that by selecting its members he would sufficiently insure the subservience of the judiciary.[14]

While the Maupeou reforms moved in a modern direction, they followed the traditional path as well. Two metaphorical statements made by the chancellor in his compte rendu clearly show that he was thinking of reform in two conceptually different ways. In speaking of reforms that he would have made in civil procedure, had he only been granted the opportunity, he said: "My project was of submitting it to a severe revision, of cutting the root of new abuses." But in discussing his programs for the criminal law, he testified: "I am not of those who believe that all that which is old is corrupt practice and who suddenly take the axe to the foot of the tree because the tree does not always bear propitious fruits."[15]

If one examines the reforms that Maupeou was given the chance to make, one finds the same ambiguity. The parlements were returned to their original mission as the instruments of royal justice by destroying the appearance of a special relationship to the crown that had made them so feared and effective as such instruments. The reduction in the size of ressorts, to bring justice once again close to the people, was accomplished by erecting new courts, the conseils supérieurs, that were to be regarded by the people as parlements. Yet they were not named parlements nor did they have that special role in the promulgation and preservation of the law that defined the parlements. The number of officers was cut back to the efficient levels presumably characteristic of the prevenal regime by purging judges who would not go along with the crown's high-handed methods; political, not professional, criteria were applied to the selection of the Maupeou magistrates.

The confusion between traditional and modern aims in Maupeou's reforms had serious consequences for the program's chances for survival. How well the new courts functioned is a matter of some debate. Though apparently they never gained full acceptance, their existence, at least, was acknowledged by most people in fairly short order. What was more telling was the general intellectual opposition to them on constitutional grounds. Here, Voltaire was in a distinct minority. The literature attacking the Maupeou reforms from the constitutional standpoint was enormous. Typical was the prominent lawyer Guy-Jean-Baptiste Target's incredulous observation that Maupeou had seemed to place "the magistrates composing the ancient and essential body of the nation, the magistrates charged, along with the princes of the blood and the peers of the realm, with the verification and the maintenance of the laws ... on the same level [as] *hongrieurs* ['gelders'], *inspecteurs de porcs* and *contrôleurs des perruques* ['supervisors of wigs']," "unworthy" offices, the abolition of which never occasioned a second thought on the part of the monarchy. "They speak," he said, "of suppressing these magistrates with a flippancy that I cannot conceive."[16]

Although the remodeled parlements retained the right of remonstrance, they had been so cowed that no one could imagine that they would ever make forceful use of it. The nation would thus be left without any barrier against despotism. The new Parlement of Paris, in the words of Target, was "an illusion that will veil despotism, and I know of nothing more dangerous."[17] The crown, by attempting to restore the judiciary to its original position, before the "new ideas," according to Maupeou, had taken hold,[18] at the same time as it sought to align the judiciary with the emerging ideals for a court system, only succeeded in making the worst possible impression on many of the most influential people in the kingdom. The dismantling of the Maupeou reforms and the recalling of the old parlements in 1774 may very well have been seen by Turgot as the necessary first step toward winning the confidence of people in the reforms he hoped to make.[19]

But if the Maupeou program was itself a *plan réglé manqué,* it was an adumbration of many ideas to come for other plans réglés. It had also brought the subject of the parlements squarely into the arena of

7. *Allegorical Engraving Made on the Occasion of the Expulsion of the Members of the Conseil supérieur from Rouen in 1774.* Anonymous.

debate. Neither of these facts has been sufficiently appreciated by historians. Maupeou showed that the state might be changed, and rather fundamentally, even if he also convinced Frenchmen that the changes must not be made by their monarchy. And by dealing roughly with the parlements, he brought into the open all the criticisms of them that had long been accumulating. Linguet was not the only philosophe to confront for the first time, in the years 1771–1774, his ambivalence toward the parlements and to lay bare that ambivalence in published works.

### The State of French Law Courts after the Recall of the Parlements

General rejoicing greeted the return of the old parlements in 1774. "Never has there been," wrote the playwright Beaumarchais, "a livelier, stronger, or more universal sensation. The French people have become mad with enthusiasm, and I am not at all surprised by it."[20] Behind their smug assurances that they had all along expected to be recalled, the parlementaires, too, may well have felt a great sense of relief.[21] For this had been the longest of their exiles, and the courts that had replaced them had seemed to be intended by the crown as more than temporary substitutes. It had also been the first brought to an end by the death of a king.

However relieved they were to be returning, the parlementaires must have done so with a certain measure of apprehension, too. Writing in 1773, when the Maupeou reforms, such as they were, were fully wrought, Diderot summarized their effects for the empress of Russia. "The public order, or our government," he said, "has been so perfectly destroyed that I do not think that the whole power and the infinite goodness of the king . . . could reestablish it. Confidence is lost. At present, judges and other owners of offices know that they are nothing."[22] It is unlikely that such a loss of confidence was restored by a single act.

The Maupeou years had been a disheartening time for the lower courts as well. Resenting their superiors though they might, the bailliage and présidial judges could only expect their eventual, indeed imminent, return. When this or other reasons for caution or misgiving led some among these courts to withhold their approval from, or even to combat, the edicts of the crown, the chancellor showed such a lack of scruples in his counteractions toward them

LE RETOUR DU PARLEMENT

*Louis XVI, Ipsié sur sa vertu relève la justice qui ramene la Félicité publique*

8. *Le retour du Parlement (1774)*, by Jean-Bernard Restout le fils.

that even the worst malpractices of Louis XIV must have seemed minor in comparison. After the members of the Présidial of Blois, for example, resigned in protest over the edicts, the chancellor abolished their offices and created new ones to sell. (He had not ended the venality of offices in the lower courts.) Since the new judges thus bought their offices from the crown rather than from the old judges, the latter lost the whole value of their investments.[23] The hopes for timely redress of their grievances that Chancellor d'Aguesseau had so assiduously instilled in the lower court judges now seemed most unjustified. If some of these judges perceived advantages to themselves in the breaking of the parlements, many more of them must surely have seen their own evident powerlessness as well.

The conciliatory policies of the new keeper of the seals, Hue de Miromesnil, probably went some way toward salving the injured sensibilities of the parlementaires. Miromesnil, as *premier président* of the Parlement of Rouen, had been one of the most spirited, if reasonable, opponents of Maupeou and had proudly rejected the latter's offer of the position of premier président in the remodeled Parlement of Paris in 1771. Instead he had set forth in 1772 his moderate views on the terms by which the parlements might be brought back.[24] This, together with his having become close friends with Maurepas during his exile, made him the natural choice for director of the magistrature during the new monarch's reign.[25]

Miromesnil had admitted, in his work of 1772, that the parlements prior to Maupeou had stood in need of reform. "The judges," he had said, "were not guaranteed as they should have been from the general corruption; interest and ambition seduced a great number of them; they abandoned the noble simplicity of their fathers; the love of a glorious industriousness vanished; they neglected study and lost from sight their ancient discipline." He had furthermore indicated his openness to plans for making justice more easily available to the people, as by creating more parlements. But in general, he had stated, it was his belief that the old parlements could have been reformed without destroying them. "Monarchical government," he had declared, "is by its nature a moderate government. It should be something between despotism, which destroys everything, including the security even of the sovereign, and anarchy, which reverses all and which casts a cruel uncertainty over the state of private persons."[26]

When he became keeper of the seals, he tried to keep the monarchy on this middle course, and until the late 1780s, when talk of crushing the parlements again began in earnest, the sovereign court judges may well have been losing much of their apprehension. The period of Miromesnil's administration may indeed have begun to seem to them a return to purely traditional reform on the part of the crown, while unsettling schemes for modern reform, at least with respect to the judiciary, became for the first time the cause only of those outside the royal government.

It was, in general, a temporizing policy that Miromesnil pursued toward the lower courts, too. Here, however, it would seem to have been rather less successful in repairing the damage done by Maupeou. One reason was that he did not apply the policy consistently. Among the numerous, pained cries from the présidiaux in August 1777, when Miromesnil "modified" his earlier 1774 edict raising the jurisdictional limits of these courts,[27] was one recorded by the Présidial of Vitry-le-François in Champagne.[28] In a printed commentary of some fifty pages, the Vitry judges went through the 1777 edict article by article, showing how each was contrary to both the spirit and the letter of the sixteenth-century legislation establishing the présidiaux.

The sections of the edict restricting the présidiaux from ever rendering final judgment in some kinds of cases, as, for instance, those regarding manufactories and hospitals, commercial disputes even in small towns (jurisdiction over which had supposedly been returned to the présidiaux by an edict of 1759), and many feudal matters, and from passing final judgment in all other kinds of cases unless specifically requested to do so by the parties involved, were denounced by the judges. "The edict of creation of the présidial jurisdiction," they said, "attributes to it the cognizance of all civil cases, without exception, up to . . . [the designated amount], in the last resort." "The king, who wanted to impede his subjects from ruining themselves by taking appeals over small matters to the sovereign courts," they furthermore argued, "did not leave to the dispositions of the litigants the recourse to the jurisdiction that he had instituted in this design. The edict of 1777 gives on the contrary . . . the liberty of using or not using the présidial jurisdiction, adverse to the principle until then inviolable, that jurisdictions are of public law and that it lies within the discretion neither of the judges nor the parties to invert the order and elude the authority of it." The judges concluded by saying that the 1777 edict could render the présidial competence a "chimera"; they reminded the king of "the degree of abandonment of judicial offices in the provinces, the lack of officers, the nonexistence of incentives and prerogatives that could make the companies whole"; and they asked "whether the edict of 1777 would revive in the provinces the vocation to the magistrature."

The crown soon retracted many parts of this edict. One wonders, though, whether there had not been behind the 1777 edict not only the forceful lobbying of the parlements against the présidiaux, but also a lingering, modern ambition on the part of the crown to consolidate jurisdictions, in this case by phasing out altogether the présidial distinction held by some of the bailliages. Speaking of the présidiaux in the preamble to the 1777 edict, Miromesnil had described the "difficulties concerning the nature and value of matters susceptible of being judged présidialement" as well as the lack of proper subordination of the présidiaux in respect to the parlements, "their legitimate and natural superiors."[29] One gets a sense, from reading this preamble, that there may have been a philosophical as well as a political motive to the chancellor's action. The realities of the times, however—namely, the tide of disorder in the countryside and the need to support the lower courts to keep them in place to stem it—dictated that he soon abandon his effort and once again let out the leash of expectations on which he, like his predecessors, kept the members of the lower courts. If the leash no longer choked the présidial judges after 1778, when the edict revising in their favor the edict of 1777 was issued, it may have chafed them rather more than previously. For if the judges could hope after 1778 that better things might yet be in store, and if that hope was sufficient to keep most of the remaining judges at their posts, they cannot have served without a certain bitterness and, like the parlementaires, a wariness of this crown that had once tried to do away with them.

Another reason for the relative lack of success of the crown in winning back the lower-court officers was that even when the crown was genuinely trying to improve the situation of these officers it did not address itself to the full range of the causes of their disaffection. Chief among these issues were the reorganizations of the *municipalités*, begun in 1692 and consummated between 1764 and 1772, which had sharply reduced the prerogatives and influence of bailliage judges in local government. A group of memorials submitted by the Présidial of Auxerre to Feydeau de Brou (Charles-Henri, grandson of the former keeper of the seals), Intendant of Burgundy, in July 1783 shows clearly the concerns that these reorganizations had prompted in the minds of the judges.[30]

Deprived first, in 1692, of their long-held right to name the *maire* ("mayor") of their city from among the members of their company (when that position was made an *office* and promptly snapped up by the Estates of Burgundy), the judges of Auxerre also found themselves individually barred in 1772 from the post of *premier échevin* ("first alderman"), the second most important appointment in their city and one of which they claimed to have been in corporate possession "since time immemorial."[31] The municipal reforms of 1764, they explained, had provided for a new *corps de ville*, composed of elected notables, conseillers, échevins, and maire, with the members of the présidial eligible still both to participate fully in the election and to hold any position. In 1771 the king had turned all the new positions back into *charges*—"having recognized . . . the inconveniences attached to elections"—but still left open the possibility to members of the présidial of acquiring the charges. The *élus* ("tax administrators") of the province, however, immediately acquired them all, and in 1772 the ordonnance was issued that limited the city offices of conseiller and above to "avocats, physicians, procureurs, notaires, surgeons, merchants, and bourgeois." "The officers of the bailliage," said the amazed judges, "were forgotten . . . This exclusion . . . is unprecedented." "It was just, one can even say that it was indispensable," argued the judges, "that the first corps of the city concur with the municipal administration. It is like that that one thought for several centuries." But now, they said, they were specifically barred from city government.

And not only had they been barred from the government, but they were also faced with being altogether excluded from the *police* of Auxerre. Here the judges were able to identify not only as the beneficiary of but also as the moving force behind this possible transfer of power their inveterate rival, the Burgundian estates. As the judges told the story, soon after the estates had bought the office of maire in 1692, the king had joined the police of Auxerre—formerly shared between the présidial and the prévôt of the city—to the mairie.[32] Thus in the space of eight years, the présidial had lost two of the chief attributes of its civic preeminence, and both to the estates. The présidial retained, however, the right to adjudicate appeals from the mairie, and from 1764 to 1771 it had once again the opportunity to obtain the mairie itself, though it did not. Even after 1772, when the présidial had seemingly lost the mairie for good, the judges could assert themselves in their community by passing on the sentences and other actions of the mairie.

But in 1783 the judges wrote to Feydeau about a recent decision of the king's council to shift cognizance of appeals from the Mairie of Macon from the présidial of that city to the parlement (of Paris, for this part of Burgundy). This decision, they said, had inspired the estates to demand that the council do the same with respect to Auxerre, and they were afraid that the council would comply with the demand. Referring to the proposal as "a project of revolution so contrary to [our] rights," the Présidial of Auxerre declared "that the right of cognizance over the police of [our] city cannot be removed from [us] without denaturing the offices of the bailliage and without substantially hurting the property of the officeholders." Here again, however, one wonders whether the projected actions of the king's council were motivated only by the lobbying of the Burgundian estates, or also by a modern desire of the crown to confine the courts to strictly legal matters.

With another proposal in the wind during 1783—the suppression of the four positions of *conseiller honoraire* that had been attached to their company since 1668, when the *élection* of Auxerre was abolished, to render justice in the matter of *aides* and *tailles*—the judges of the Auxerre court found themselves in agreement.[33] What catches one's attention in reading the judges' discussion of the proposal is the following statement:

> If . . . [the officers of the présidial] thought that the revolution on the way [the suppression of the positions of conseiller honoraire] could be disadvantageous to . . . [the conseillers honoraires], far from soliciting it, they would join their prayers to impede it; but they do not think even that these officers [the conseillers honoraires] have a true interest in opposing it. One could not refuse to them an advantageous liquidation, which will take the place for them of the sale of their offices in a time when the offices of the judicature are in discredit.

Their prediction of a submissive reaction from the conseillers honoraires to the abolition of their offices was a correct analysis of the attitude that the judges themselves would take, in just a few years, toward the liquidation of their own offices during a much more sweeping revolution.

The acquiescence of judges in the abolition of their offices during the Revolution, and in the ending of the Old Regime as a whole, was perfectly understandable. If the crown had checked its modern impulses with respect to the jurisdictional limits of the présidiaux after 1778, it continued to follow a bewilderingly ambiguous policy with respect to the municipal role of these courts. If it had prevented the présidial offices from falling into worse discredit, it had not removed them from existing discredit. If it had repaired the superficial damage done to the présidial courts by Maupeou and temporarily relieved the anxieties among their members that Maupeou's reforms had so intensified, the crown had not set itself on a course that would insure that those anxieties would not arise again. On the contrary, the course that Miromesnil followed could only have had, in the long run, the most baleful effects on the judges' morale and, by extension, on the strength of judicial institutions and the ability of the crown to govern. With regard to parlements, if Miromesnil's ministry had given them grounds for complacency, the ministry of his successor, Lamoignon de Basville, only brought back in a rush all the agonizing memories of the Maupeou years. The resulting, and by degrees even greater, demoralization of the parlementaires quickly manifested itself in a lack of commitment to the very survival of the monarchy.

Before turning from the judges to some of the other proponents of court reform in French society during the 1770s and 1780s, one might consider the last in the group of memorials sent by the Présidial of Auxerre to the Intendant of Burgundy in 1783, this one concerning the state of the building in which the présidial judges held their court.[34] Not limiting themselves to complaints about the poor way in which the building was maintained by the city, the judges also decried the floor plan of their palais. "The criminal chamber," they said,

is in a . . . bizarre situation. Its door is in the courtroom; the criminals that one conducts without cease into this chamber and who are often shackled are obliged to traverse the council chamber and the *grande salle*, to their great humiliation. They attract all eyes to them, and frequently it happens that the session is interrupted by the noise of their passage. If the judges are . . . assembled in the council chamber, the inconvenience is not less; they see without necessity the unhappy prisoners pass and repass before their eyes; the sound of the doors and the racket of the chains suspend their attention and can only produce prejudicial effects.

The judges were requesting that the crown improve their palais not because their vanity was offended, but because it was not allowing them to perform their responsibilities toward the accused professionally and fairly. Though feeling beleaguered by their rivals and forgotten by the crown, the lower-court judges did not, even as the Old Regime crumbled, cease to envision a set of professional guidelines in accordance with the new ideals of their century.

5 / Views toward the Reconstruction of the

Judiciary on the Eve of Revolution

The unreliable and weakened state of the French courts resum-
moned in 1774 made further attempts at comprehensive judicial reform imperative for the crown. It made it just as certain, though,
that the crown could not make such attempts without putting
everything in total disarray, which was in fact what it did in 1788.
Having aroused great suspicions against itself during the Maupeou
years, the crown could only confirm those suspicions by moving once
more against the parlements; having shaken so severely all the nor-
mal expectations of its judges, it could not count on their support
should its efforts to make a new judiciary once more fail.

If the crown, however, was inhibited from reforming the courts
after 1774, many in French society were encouraged as never before,
by the experiment of 1771–1774, to think about what judicial reforms might be desirable. Furthermore, the last barriers to the con-
fluence of currents that would form the revolutionaries' ideas for a
new judiciary seemed to have been broken down. The later writings
of Linguet, Guyton de Morveau, Servan, and Jousse, the contribu-
tions of newcomers like Bernardi, Pétion de Villeneuve, and Barbat
du Closel d'Arnery, the entries in the essay competition sponsored
by the Academy of Châlons-sur-Marne in 1782 on ways to increase
the speed and reduce the costs of justice, and the cahiers drawn up
for the meeting of the Estates-General in 1789 all contributed to a
veritable profusion of works on court reform in the 1770s and 1780s.
And with the example that Maupeou had set, or almost set, of reforming the parlements too, few of these works failed to include the
parlements in their schemes as well. Some, in fact, went so far when
they treated supreme, regional courts as to omit even the name *parlement,* suggesting that the court system they envisioned was to be
wholly different from the one they had. Maupeou's actions, by
showing that a new system might be instituted, had provided not
only the sanction, apparently, but also the shock that released many

minds from the existing world and let them wander to realms of the imagination.

### Critiques of Royal Reform and Fresh Insights
### into the Shortcomings of the Judiciary

Different inspirations for French reformers in the 1770s and 1780s were the legislation of other European princes, notably those of Prussia, Austria, and Tuscany (which was itself, ironically, inspired in part by that of Louis XIV); the observations of laws and institutions made on trips, real or imagined, to distant, particularly Oriental, lands; and the exigencies of economic change and growth in population. The content of the reformers' proposals indicates, however, that it was inspired mainly by the indigenously developing ideas for court reform that Maupeou's actions had caused to spring forth. While economic and social pressures may have pushed reformers to accentuate one or another aspect of their proposals, the essential shape of the proposals was fashioned in accord with the geometrical dictates of modern reform. The links between the thoughts that Saint-Pierre, d'Aguesseau, and d'Argenson, for example, had had about reform and the proposals put forward in the post-Maupeou years are quite clear. It may be seen also that a major objection to Maupeou's reform was that it did not sufficiently embody the objectives of a modern judicial reform.

Writing in 1777, Linguet said that "impartial theorizers . . . hoping from a revolution some remedy for abuses become intolerable in the judicial order," had been prepared in 1771 to lend their support to "a legislator occupied with the good of the nation."[1] Seeing, though, that "the precipitation and incapacity of Chancellor Maupeou had . . . prevented this reform from acquiring a firm consistency," these theorizers, Linguet implied, had withheld their support. The reform had not taken steps toward "correcting procedure, expediting formalities, [and] repressing the vexations of lawyers."[2] It had not been, in other words, a comprehensive, integrated, truly modern reform.

Linguet went on, in his work of 1777, to review the proposals for court reform that he had advanced in 1771, proposals almost identical, in the way they would have altered the relationship between the parlements and the présidiaux, to the legislation authored by La-

moignon de Basville in 1788. Commenting on the unsuitability of
the conseils supérieurs as replacements for the parlements, Linguet
stated:

It is in vain that one would compensate for the defection [of the parlements] by
forming new bodies on which one would lavish the same attributes ... Even if
these new companies were a hundred times more just, a hundred times more enlightened [than the parlements], they would not be any less the object of public
aversion, because in the eyes of contemporaries their birth will always be stigma-
tized by the idea of illegitimacy. But there exist ... in this realm a hundred
[présidiaux], consecrated by time, recognized by the parlements themselves, after
some long badgerings ... Give to them the right of judging all criminal cases in
the last resort, on appeal from the bailliages, and civil affairs, too, up to the
amount of twenty, of thirty thousand francs; you will be forever safe from the incursions of the parlements [on the royal authority]; the course of justice will no
longer suffer ... from any interruption ... There then is a resource taken away
from the parlements when they would like to mutinee: the murmurings of the
peoples ... That way, without expense, without exertion, without labor, you will
register a blow to the parlementary confederation from which it will never rise
again.[3]

The reader notes in these proposals Linguet's awareness of public
opinion, his sense not only of the limits that it placed on lawmakers,
but also of the uses to which it might be put. But one also sees how
abstract and ahistoric, really, Linguet's proposals were. If Linguet
heeded the voices of the people, he had in mind rather idealized,
malleable people who would suddenly be satisfied with an efficient
administration of justice. If he urged the king to make use of the existing institutions of the présidiaux, he did not have in mind the
présidiaux that Henry II had created, those extra competences of
some selected bailliages and sénéchaussées to provide people with
final justice closer to home and to regulate the flow of cases to the
overburdened parlements. He had in mind institutions that fit a
geometrical plan for a judiciary concerned only with the administration of justice, from which the old parlements, established in historical provinces and possessing prerogatives and functions acquired
through slow accretion over time, would be all but excluded.

If Linguet advocated modern reform during the last two decades
before the Revolution, he was not alone. This period saw indeed the
full flowering of modern reform. The harbingers of this occurrence
appeared in the 1760s. In the eulogy of d'Aguesseau that he delivered before the French academy in 1760, Antoine Léonard Thomas
said that what he meant to laud most in the chancellor who had

died eight years earlier was his "returning all the way to the *source du mal* in reforming the laws." Previous "great men who had occupied themselves with legislation" had "sought rather to correct abuses than to establish principles"; Saint Louis "prepared a revolution and did not make it."[4] "The greatest, the most beautiful characteristic of legislation," stated Thomas, "is unity of principles: departing always from the same ideas, tending toward the same end, establishing a general harmony between all laws, adapting itself so well to a people that it belongs to them just as their moral practices, their soil, and their climate. That of France never had this character. It was nearly always a formless hotchpotch of contending laws."[5]

The influence that distinguished d'Aguesseau from his predecessors in his approach to legislation was, in the view of Thomas, that of Descartes. In the notes to his eulogy, Thomas described how the chancellor, as a youth, had been made to read at first "allegedly philosophical works, where one uttered, under the name of Aristotle, nonsense that this philosopher had never said. A spirit like that of d'Aguesseau was not made to content itself with that. As soon as one put Descartes between his hands he sensed at once the difference. He admired the advantages of this method, which, in departing from a self-evident point leads to an assured proof. Thereafter he always made use of it, be it for instructing himself, be it for convincing others."[6] And it was not just d'Aguesseau whom Thomas saw as having been guided by Descartes, but also every important thinker and writer since the 1650s: "He guided equally Pascal and Corneille, Locke and Bourdaloue, Newton and Montesquieu." "The spirit of Descartes is everywhere," said Thomas in his 1765 panegyric of the philosopher himself. "One has admitted it to the arts and letters as well as to the sciences." It was, furthermore, an influence of which Thomas approved thoroughly, saying that he looked forward eagerly to its being exerted at last on "legislation and the government of states."[7]

The jurist and former member of the Cour des monnaies of Lyon, Jussieu de Montluel, asked in 1761, "For what can one not hope in a century where everything perfects itself?"[8] The year before, he had published a book that became very popular, *Instruction facile sur les conventions; ou, Notions simples sur les divers engagemens qu'on peut prendre dans la société.* Following the example of Domat, he had endeavored in this work to explain the subject of contracts so clearly, starting from simple definitions that would be accessible to anyone, that people would no longer need lawyers to help them enter into agreements with their fellows.[9] In a treatise of 1771 that was the culmination of a series of discourses that he had delivered in the 1760s, mainly before the Parlement of Burgundy, the lawyer-chemist-encyclopedist Guyton de Morveau chided "those who clung still to local customs on the basis of some pretended relation between them and morality."[10] To know all that was wrong with French laws, Guyton asserted, in fine modern fashion, "It is necessary to have followed often the scale of legal consequences to the principles of moral law, to the immutable truths of moral interest, of public interest, of civil interest, which serve as their base, and to have found in our diverse laws these principles and these interests in opposition."[11]

Some did object to modern reform and the mechanistic approach to government and social organization for which the sensationalist and materialist philosophies of Helvétius, La Mettrie, d'Holbach, and others seemed to provide further underpinning. Voltaire had roundly denounced Saint-Pierre for thinking that society could be reordered through law. Only moral education, "enlightenment," internal regeneration, in the view of Voltaire, could "cure the diseases of superstition and intolerance."[12] The chevalier de Chastellux, in advice somewhat later to the newly independent people in America, "urged [them] ... not to place their faith in institutional change, but rather in the development of learning."[13] The universal applicability of any one method even in the sciences was attacked. Buffon and Diderot, for instance, noted that a method that worked in mathematics was not necessarily of any help in botany.[14]

Even among critics of the mechanistic approach to politics, however, one finds a modern desire for orderliness. In praising the work of Colbert in his *Siècle de Louis XIV*, Voltaire wrote: "Uniformity in all kinds of administration is a virtue."[15] It must also be admitted that by continually pointing to what he saw as the vicious, cruel, senseless aspects of human institutions, by ridiculing the Panglossian complacency that maintained them, Voltaire probably did as much as anyone to support the case for modern reform. Chastellux, for his part—in a famous work admired by Voltaire on the causes of public happiness—criticized the institutions of property, which he said had led to undesirable inequalities. He also wrote a eulogy of Helvétius in 1774.[16] One could argue, in fact, that these critics of the mechanistic approach were even more modern than its self-avowed advocates, that they did not want to stop with institutional change but meant to go all the way to the very nature of men and change that. Be that as it may, one will note here simply the tentative resolution achieved by two reformers in the decades before the Revolution, Marmontel and Servan.

In his popular work of 1767, *Bélisaire,* the sentimental moralist and tragedian Jean-François Marmontel had his long-suffering, virtuous hero discuss with Justinian the emperor Constantine's decision to move the capital of the empire. Belisarius disapproved of the decision, although it was impelled by a motive with which he sympathized. The emperor's motive was to achieve a reform of the empire. He thought that this could most effectively be achieved by starting anew in a different location. In so doing, he both went to more trouble than was necessary and failed to accomplish what he sought. He did not see that "at Rome only one good reign was needed to change the face of things."[17] "How much is it to be lamented," said Belisarius, "that so enlarged a genius, with all that firmness, that spirit of enterprise, should egregiously mistake the fitness of the means to produce the end desired, and exert for the extinction of the empire more vigour and activity than would have been necessary to retrieve its ancient honours!" And in expending so much effort on this needless task of moving the capital, Constantine was unable to continue and complete those administrative and social reforms that he had begun so promisingly at Rome. The result was "a mere theatrical shifting of scenery."

It is necessary, Belisarius had his gardener say, to weed rather than lop off noxious plants. Applied to the government of states, however, this did not mean that one should pursue a policy of wholesale destruction. For a state cannot be re-created in a moment: the creation of a state "requires the progressive toil of ages, the slow and imperceptible working of sentiment, habit, and opinion." And if the good characteristics of a state take time to develop, so the bad ones, too, establish themselves over time. Legislation may help—and Belisarius called for reforms in the administration of justice, to be realized chiefly by the rewriting of complex collections of statutes and customs into "a few good laws, simple, clear, sensible, and easy in their application to the actions of men." But legislation can only go so far. Laws alone will not change contrary "sentiment, habit, and opinion." On the other hand, Belisarius exclaimed, "how rapid would be their fall!" if the monarch were to provide by his conduct a superior moral example for his subjects. Were he to make the honorable, the industrious, and the frugal the standards of his conduct, he would make them at once the models for his people. Changes in the constitution, the institutions, the laws, the location of the capital of a state could by themselves probably never correct the course of that state, but the example of the sovereign might transform it in the twinkling of an eye.

That these ideas were less contradictory than they seem may perhaps be understood better by looking at the way in which Servan fit them together. He also believed that the example set by the king was of paramount importance. "Whereas under firm princes," he said, comparing the reign of Louis XIV with the state of France during the Wars of Religion, "everything is motive for obeying, everything under feeble princes becomes pretext for revolt and germ of revolution."[18] But for him the laws were also a matter of great concern. It was, in his mind, imperative that the laws be reformed, which for him meant that they be better defined and organized, regularized and moderated.

In a work published just one year after Beccaria's much admired *Dei delitti e della pene* became available in French translation, the young Servan, recently become avocat général in the Parlement of Grenoble, called for legislatively prescribed sentences. "Every day," he said, "the judges deliberate on whether they should condemn a criminal to the galleys for a time or for life; the laws are mute, it is necessary to supplement them."[19] He called for the scientific determination of sentences, the exact balancing in them of the social good and the welfare of the condemned; and he also explained how this determination might be made. "In general," he said, "the spirit of all good criminal law is to reconcile as much as possible the least punishment of the guilty with the greatest public utility. The indivisible point where these two things meet is the only one that is necessary to mark. A right reason, aided by a sensitive heart, would infallibly succeed in discovering it."[20] The debt to Beccaria is quite evident, but also clear is the relation of Servan's thought (indeed, like Becarria's) to the developing consensus of French reformers in favor of a rational, systematic rewriting of the law.

In his more mature works of the 1780s, Servan went into greater detail about how the "right reason" of which he spoke was to be informed. He criticized the "schools of the north," the works of Wolff, Grotius, and Puffendorf. Wolff had "overloaded" his work with all the "apparatus of geometry"; Grotius and Puffendorf had just as "ridiculously decorated" theirs with "the most antiquated erudition."[21] "It seems to me," he said, "that one has too much wanted to treat moral philosophy as a science, that one has not seized its true character and that which distinguishes it from the exact sciences; too much reason, or, to say it better, a false reason, has desiccated it by applying to it a method that does not suit it, in robbing it of the strength, the grace, and the beauty that are proper to it." Ethical truths, he went on to say, could be better seen "in the plains of Paraguay or in the forests of the Mississippi, under the garb or in the nudity of a savage, than behind these bizarre ornaments." The moral science, then, that would allow the legislator precisely to determine appropriate penalties for different crimes was the knowledge of the human heart. And it was the forcefulness of moral authenticity that would give new laws built up from it (still geometrically, but more reliably so) their immediate strength. Such laws would be part and parcel of the virtuous prince's rule.

Servan, one may note parenthetically, changed his views drastically as a result of the Revolution, which he came to abhor for its excesses and atrocities. In a work of the early 1780s, he had recited the whole litany of criticisms commonly leveled against Montesquieu by pre-Revolutionary reformers. "Far from the delays, the expenses, the dangers of our justice being the price of our liberty," he had stated, "I maintain that they are an enormous salary paid for having it diminished without cease; I maintain that nearly all the slownesses of our justice come from some vices in our institutions." The venality of offices, the unnecessary degrees of jurisdiction, the confusion of competencies—all of these, in Servan's mind, had been vices and had needed correction.[22] But after watching the attempts of the Revolutionary legislators to create a wholly new state, Servan considered them horrifying failures and reverted to the very conservative position that he judged Montesquieu to have occupied. "Yes, without doubt," he now admitted, "legislation is not a confused mass of laws but a system where all the parts must stay as they are."[23]

The work in which Servan rendered his new verdict on Montesquieu was a commentary on Montaigne's *Essays* in which he approvingly discussed the essay on custom. But it was the more sophisticated, sociological conservatism of Montesquieu rather than the stoical conservatism of Montaigne that Servan was really defending. The complex interrelationships of laws and institutions made their reform, he now believed, too difficult a task for the limited abilities of men. "Instead of tormenting yourself to reform the state," he counseled the reader, "occupy yourself a moment with reforming yourself; instead of demanding with so many cries the assembly of the Estates-General, compose in your mind the assembly of your opinions, of your past actions."[24] The erstwhile reformer was still urging his fellow citizens to look into themselves, but with a penitential rather than illuminative goal. The knowledge of the heart was no longer to be made operative. Servan's cautious advice was all that was left of his great and hopeful programs, as the long neglected injunctions against using scientific methods in politics regained their authority.

### A Cornucopia from the Provinces

If the pre-Revolutionary works of Marmontel and Servan showed a graceful, conscious synthesis of the arguments of both modern reformers and their critics, other writings revealed a relatively unconscious agreement in their presuppositions about reform. Colorful and hitherto unexplored documentation of the growing consensus of opinion in French society on how the courts might be reformed may be found in the essays that survive from the 1782 competition sponsored by the Academy of Châlons-sur-Marne.[25] The Academy published its first notice of the competition in the *Gazette de France* in September 1780. The notice attracted the attention of a wide variety of people. Correspondents included a retired *greffier* ("clerk") named Goimbauls, who lived on the rue du Boeuf couronné in Poissy, and a young avocat in the Parlement of Paris named Falour du Vergier, who lived in the Cloître St. Jean.

An anonymous writer identified himself only as "your very humble and obedient servant from a small corner of a province where one does not find even good paper for writing decently." A Monsieur G. B. T. of Paris wrote in, "under seal of the greatest discretion," to ask permission to send in his essay after the deadline. He included

a preliminary outline of his projected work, a request for the program of the next contest (on "the means of rendering the lot of people in the countryside as happy as possible"; some, apparently, eagerly watched for the contests sponsored by the different academies
and enthusiastically entered as many as they could), and elaborate
instructions to the academy for addressing its reply to his letter in
care of a third party. A Monsieur Abril, *doyen des procureurs* in the
Bailliage of Arles, wrote in to ask why there had been no response to
his earlier letter offering the academy a prospectus of his forthcom-
ing work, *Lettres copthiques sur l'histoire des temps avant la création du
monde,* in which he promised to insert "an ordinance of the emperor
of Ethiopia on the reformation of justice, containing 21 chapters and
500 articles." If this extraordinary work, which Abril claimed was
the result of "an experience of fifty and even of sixty years," ever
reached the academy, no trace of it, unfortunately, seems to remain.

Among the eleven persons whose essays, or summaries of them,
survive in the archives of the academy were a conseiller in the Parlement of Bordeaux (Goyon d'Arsac, who wrote essays for nearly
twenty different academic contests, on subjects as diverse as girls'
schools, Louis XII, clothing, and language);[26] three avocats (one in
the Parlement of Toulouse, a Monsieur Gez; and two in the Parlement of Paris, a Monsieur Traullé and one of the sons of the well-
known jurist Daniel Jousse); the procureur du roi in the Présidial of
Beauvais (Louis-Jean-Baptiste Bucquet, also a writer of local histories, who won the contest);[27] a curé from Trèves named Urbain; a
"notaire royalle" from Valenciennes named Tordoir; and four
whose professions—and, in three cases, even whose names—were not
given (in the fourth case, furthermore, the entrant identified himself
only as "C. A. P."). An additional, published essay was written but
not submitted for the competition by Jérôme Pétion de Villeneuve,
avocat in the Présidial of Chartres and maire of Paris during the
Revolution.[28] The prize-winning essay by Bucquet was, of course,
also published, as was Goyon's.[29]

The essays by the curé and the notaire, first of all, may be dismissed in a few words. The academy itself did not deem either of
them to merit serious consideration. Of the former the academy's
commentator said that it offered nothing of interest and that "the
manner in which it is written makes one regret the time that one
spent in reading it"; and it was, indeed, the work of an eccentric.

Urbain proposed completely doing away with courts, judges, procureurs, avocats, and "all their libraries." He urged instead the appointment of *auditeurs* in each town to hear and decide cases and send litigants on their way. Punishments for all crimes committed by commoners would be corporal; no fines would be collected so that no one would be unable to pay his taille. If the crime were serious enough, the *roturier* might be flogged every day, "in secret or in public," for an entire month. Ecclesiastics, nobles, and "gens civilisés" would be punished by "mortifications, privations, and degradations." If one were to argue, he said, that one would be in danger of being judged badly under his system, one could respond by saying that there is always danger of that! In his system one would at least not lose the "time and money" consumed by trials.

Urbain's only trace of caution appeared in his recommendation that the system first be tried in a small province before being extended to the whole kingdom. An additional point in favor of his system, he ended by saying, was that the auditeurs would be able to assist the intendants, watch over the forests, and protect the rights of the hunt. As for the essay submitted by the notary Tordoir, which had for its *dévise,* "Le Seigneur fait miséricorde, il fait justice à ceux que l'on opprime," it was simply unintelligible. Coming from Flanders, the essay had apparently been written, the academy concluded, by a non-Frenchman.

The essay by "C. A. P.," who referred several times to practices in Brittany and so may have lived in that province, was also dismissed by the academy as deserving no attention. It was a brief and occasionally sententious piece, which opened by declaring that people should tame their passions, "the origin of all the troubles that desolate the universe." The author said that he was aware of its deficiencies, explaining that he had been for a long time in bad health. Noteworthy, though, is the fact that this essay, like the curé Urbain's, proposed submitting all cases to arbitration, although C. A. P. recommended *conciliateurs* only for civil cases and would still have had ordinary courts for the cases that could not be settled through arbitration.

To suggest arbitration was to wave a red flag before the members of the academy, not only because it seemed simple-minded to them, but also because it indicated that one did not have a due regard for the livelihood of members of their class. The academicians responded sharply to the suggestions by two of the other entrants, Gez and Bucquet, that people be given the right to plead their own *causes.* Giving people that right, they said, would "deprive avocats of the reward for which they have the right to hope from the studies and the vigils that they have consecrated to the service of the public; it would take away from the procureurs the revenue from their offices, which often they have purchased very dearly." The academicians similarly came to the defense of their class when some of the contestants, again including the prize-winning Bucquet, urged the elimination of seignorial justices. "The suppressions and changes proposed in the seignorial justices," they said, mincing no words, "appear to attack the propertied." Also worth noting, though, is the fact that both Gez and Bucquet were themselves lawyers. In the 1780s France entered that brief period in its history when politics became for a considerably larger number of people than usual separated from strict self-interest.

The other eight essays all received rather more serious consideration from the academy. That is not to say that the academy was pleased with them. Indeed, it expressed its general disappointment in them. Nearly all of the means that they put forward for expediting and reducing the costs of justice seemed either undesirable or impracticable or ineffectual to the members of the academy. In awarding the prize to Bucquet, the academicians specified that they were recognizing the "zeal and learning of a good citizen," but that they could not "pretend to see effected the reforms that he proposes." At first glance, the academicians appeared to want reforms that would maintain the judicial bourgeoisie while providing for improvement in the administration of justice. They did not seem to want reforms that implied a reorganization of the whole state, that entailed a broad restructuring of social institutions. In a word, if they seemed at times sympathetic to modern reforms, as to those proposed, for instance, by Goyon d'Arsac, they tended to see traditional reforms as more *politique.* One of the reporters for the academy noted with approval the essay by Traullé, the Parisian avocat, for, "Without touching the great objects that regard administration, it confines itself to the objects that one can remedy without inverting the judicial order, without touching general legislation." The competition was, however, a literary and scientific one, and the fair-minded academicians awarded their prize to the essay written in the most felicitous style, argued most cogently, and based on the most thorough and detailed research.

It is quite clear what the academy members regarded as undesirable or impracticable. Undesirable among Bucquet's suggestions was his idea for "prescribing a single customary law."[30] "It is dangerous to touch there," they said, "the discontent of the peoples; their attachment to ancient usages, the derangement of fortunes, the uncertainty of judgments during a long succession of years are things well capable of arresting or suspending the activity of the legislator." Impracticable among the proposals in one of the anonymous memoirs was the scheme for abolishing the venality of offices and the collection of épices by reimbursing officeholders the value of their charges and paying salaries to newly appointed judges out of the revenues of an unstated number of "gros bénéfices." The great benefices, being of "no utility" and serving "only to support the luxurious style of life of a small number of persons," would be reclaimed by the crown. (Foreshadowing what would actually be done during the Revolution, monks under this scheme would be reassigned a *subsistence* from the fonds of their monasteries.) The reporter to the academy could not quarrel with the "clarity and precision" of this section of the memoir, but he doubted that his fellow academicians would adopt "a system of which the execution would meet nearly insurmountable obstacles." Why the academicians thought some proposals ineffectual, however, is more difficult to understand. But a guess may be ventured.

In their critique of one of the other anonymous memoirs, the academicians stated that the contestant had not outlined sufficient means for making justice faster and less expensive. "The program [of the competition]," they said, "opens a field much more vast than that which the author of this memoir has traversed." "One regrets, for example," they continued, "not seeing indicated means for simplifying the procedure in the first instance." The academy members did not, in other words, find the memoir comprehensive enough. It did not start with a view of the whole system of justice, nor appreciate the full interrelationship of all its components. These shortcomings, rather than the absence of any specific recommendation, made the proposals ineffectual. The academicians seem to have taken the perspective of Montesquieu on institutions, but with the intention of reforming them, however slightly, rather than merely describing them. They seem thus to have tended in spite of themselves toward the belief in the possibility of a successful reworking of institutions to achieve certain ends that the writings of Saint-Pierre had heralded.

If the thoughts of the academicians were tinged with the shade of modern reform, those of the contestants were bathed in it. The essays that the contestants submitted to the academy suggest a very large degree of consensus among Frenchmen in the years immediately preceding the Revolution on the reforms needed in the administration of justice. "I do not fabricate a monster in order to combat it," said Bucquet, "I attack the one that is proclaimed by the public alarm."[31] "The widely-known disorders in our civil laws and in the administration of justice," wrote Pétion de Villeneuve, "have reached such a point that a general reform becomes absolutely indispensable."[32]

The reform for which the people called comprised, in the minds of the essayists, seven general principles. The first was a reduction in the number of kinds of law courts and in the levels of jurisdictions ("supprimer et réunir" was, for example, the principle of Gez) and the redistribution of the ressorts of the remaining courts according to a more or less geometrical plan. The second suggested procedural and organizational changes to facilitate the flow of cases through the courts and to insure that cases were handled fairly (for example, having only one *instruction,* or preliminary investigation, multiplying *audiences,* especially for summary matters, setting the docket on a first-come, first-serve basis, and opening up to public scrutiny all proceedings). The third called for provisions for the poor to obtain legal counsel everywhere and at all times (as it was, the poor had benefit of counsel for suits that they wished to raise only in a few scattered locales, according to the vagaries of institutional benevolence and private philanthropy); the oft-cited example of what should be extended generally was the Bureau de Charité of Lyon, which had provided legal services since the Middle Ages.[33] The fourth was a sharp diminution in the number of subordinate, "parasitic" court officers (and even, occasionally, the abolition *en bloc* of procureurs). The fifth proposed the elimination, or the restriction to feudal and manorial cases or to very minor, local squabbles, of the seignorial courts. The sixth commended the writing of a single customary law or code for all of France. And the seventh urged the end of the venality of offices and the collection of épices. The elimination of exceptions of all sorts was almost a mania with the essayists. Bringing all aspects of the courts within the purview of the law—a newly-worked, rational law—was the means by which the essayists believed their desire for uniformity could be satisfied.

Not every memoir, of course, covered every part of the projected general reform, but among the eight memoirs that the academy perused no part would have been greatly incompatible. Goyon d'Arsac's contribution was by some degrees the most consistently modern of the memoirs. Its keynote might have been taken from Domat. "The civil laws," said Goyon, "considered in themselves, should be only the development of the natural laws and their equitable application to the diverse circumstances that give rise among men to the state of society." "Linked to each other by a mutual harmony," he continued, "clear, precise, and distinct, the civil laws, likewise all other types of positive law, should be the simple and uniform enunciations of the public reason."

Goyon found the problems with the administration of justice in the nature of the civil laws and jurisprudence, in the form of the instruction and civil procedure, in the constitution of the courts and the magistrature, and in the unfortunate, fundamental influence of the treasury on the operation of justice. His sensibilities were revolted by the incongruity of the "enormous and undigested collection of regulations that pass for laws" in the most "powerful, enlightened, sensitive, and capable" of all the European nations, above all in "the century of reason and of philosophy." "The sages," he said, "recognized it: the edifice of our laws, this shapeless, fallen mass, is truly irreparable. The surest and perhaps the quickest course of action would be to destroy it from top to bottom, if not all at once, at least successively, and to raise instead, on a general and uniform plan, the diverse parts of a new French code."

But even in some of the less explicitly systematic memoirs, for example Traullé's and young Jousse's, one finds statements of a kind that would not have occurred two hundred years earlier. The somewhat rambling, historical essay, or, better, exposé, of Traullé is epitomized by this indictment by the author of previous reforms: "The reforms that one has made up till now have never produced great benefits; they have removed abuses only to let others appear in their place . . . We have not found among us any of those great and beautiful laws that are the glory of humanity; nothing is vast, noble, and harmonious in our legislation; all is small, all is ordinary; principles thrown everywhere at random announce neither wisdom nor profundity." And the rather indirect, if superbly organized, treatise of Jousse, who told the academy that he had "worked under the eyes of a father known for diverse works of jurisprudence and who furnished ... much help on this subject," was replete with calls for "fixing by a general rule" different aspects of judicial administration and criticism of "the variety and uncertainty" that one currently found in the administration.

The part of the desired general reform most obviously prompted by the reforms of Maupeou involved changing the types of jurisdictions and redrawing ressorts. Goyon and Pétion provided the fullest plans for these transformations. Goyon would first of all have made a clear division between ordinary and extraordinary justice. The ordinary courts, which would handle not only matters already in the ambit of the regular tribunals but also affairs dealt with by many of the smaller exceptional tribunals, including the amirautés, prévôts des marchands, prévôts des maréchaux, and the eaux et forêts, would be of three degrees. The lowest would consist of the seignorial courts, "if they survived," and the minor royal jurisdictions; the next would be that of the présidiaux, since all the bailliages and sénéchaussées would be elevated to the présidial level; and the highest would comprise the parlements and conseils souverains. The extraordinary courts, in which would be consolidated the authority of the major exceptional courts, the cours des aides, chambres des comptes, and cours des monnaies, would be of only two kinds: *sièges subsidiaires* and *cours domaniales*.

Second, Goyon would have redivided the kingdom into standard ressorts for the new courts, according to a mathematical formula. The 56,250-square league area of the country would be divided into 36 regions of 1562 square leagues, each of which would be further divided into 36 districts of 43 square leagues, which would be more finely divided into a number of arrondissements to be determined by local needs. A parlement and a cour domaniale, each with 48 judges, would sit in each 1562-square league region; a présidial and a siège subsidiaire, each with 15 judges, would serve each 43-square league district; and a seignorial or minor royal court, composed of 3 officers, would be in each arrondissement. No jurisdictions would overlap; all would have definite assignments. "By this means," said

Goyon, "the competence of the diverse tribunals will no longer be equivocal, entangled, uncertain: a fixed and well-marked line would separate not only the ordinary from the extraordinary jurisdiction, but also the different degrees of each of them, in order that the power and authority of each seat, in their mutual relations, would be determined with a clarity, a precision exactly appropriate for maintaining good order and facilitating the administration of justice."

Pétion's plan was only slightly less radical than Goyon's and would also have left little untouched. In his view, the jurisdictions of all the exceptional courts should be reunited with those of the ordinary courts. This would "greatly diminish the number of tribunals and judicial officers." Likewise, all seignorial ressorts should be joined to the ressorts of royal courts. "The time has come at last," he said, to abolish these last remnants of feudal oligarchy. Second, the ordinary courts should be of three degrees, but of three degrees only. The lowest would be constituted by *tribunaux inférieurs*, which would judge all cases in the first instance. They would have three judges and jurisdiction over an arrondissement of "four leagues or thereabouts." Six or seven of these arrondissements would compose the ressort of each *tribunal du second ordre*, which would have twelve judges. Justice of the highest degree would be exercised by *tribunaux suprêmes*, each to be staffed with forty judges. One tribunal suprême would be situated in each province. All courts were to be as near as possible to the center of their jurisdictions, "in order that justice distributes itself everywhere with an equal facility, an equal promptitude." Courts should be in "just proportions" to the needs of the state. Comparing the state to a machine and the courts to springs, Pétion said that having either too many or too few courts would keep the state from "working" properly.[34]

Even the names of the old courts were to be forgotten; Pétion's system of justice was to be almost entirely new. It was less radical than Goyon's only in its designation of the traditional provinces rather than new, geometrical divisions as the ressorts of the supreme courts, and its allowance for an adjustment in the number of judges in these courts according to the size of their provinces. "There are large provinces, there are small ones," he said.[35] Goyon would have allowed an exception to the number of forty-eight judges for each parlement only in the case of the court sitting in Paris.

Also encouraged, undoubtedly, by Maupeou's reforms were the proposals in many of the memoirs for ending the venality of offices and putting judges on strict salaries. Indeed the failure of Lamoignon de Basville's reform of 1788 to address the question of venality was one reason for its not capturing the imagination and gaining the support of more of the French people.[36] The point has already been argued, however: modern reform reached its full development in the years after the Maupeou reform and probably largely as a result of the example set by that reform. No aspect of the judiciary was any longer outside the scope of reformist treatises.

Other works from the 1780s showed the same desire for a general reform of the courts. Bernardi de Valernes, an avocat from Marseilles and another occasional contributor to academic contests, published an essay on French law in 1785 to which he appended a proposal for restoring the divisions of ancient France in order to remedy the disorders of justice. He used the divisions during the time of Charlemagne—the *comté,* the *centaine,* and the *dixaine*—more as a point of reference, however, than as a model. The reform that he suggested was almost wholly modern. "After having divided the realm into districts of nearly equal extent, relative nevertheless to their state and to their population," he said, "one would subdivide them again into districts of a lesser extent. Each district would be subordinate to a city of the first, of the second, or of the third order."[37]

The administrative units of the early Middle Ages could, it is true, be construed as having been somewhat geometrical, but it was a new ideal seen reflected in old forms rather than the power of the old forms themselves that attracted Bernardi. A line of demarcation should anyway be recognized in deciding what is traditional reform and what is romanticism or utopianism. For reformers in the sixteenth century to want to go back to the thirteenth—a distant time, to be sure, but not one with which all ties had been broken—was one thing. But for someone in the eighteenth century to demand that the kingdom be taken back to the eighth was quite another.(The drawing of examples from classical antiquity would have to be exempted from such a rule, and could be by arguing that they constituted at all times part of the immediate moral tradition of reformers during the Old Regime.)

Another avocat, Barbat du Closel d'Arnery—"who devoted himself to dreaming about social reform"—made similar proposals in a work published in the midst of and as a response to Lamoignon's experiment.[38] The reform of the keeper of the seals, though well intentioned, was defective in several respects, in the view of Barbat du Closel. It did not abolish the venality of judicial offices, first of all, nor the accompanying, "perpetual irremovability" of judges. Second, it gave the same courts, the new grands bailliages, both original and final jurisdiction in many cases. And last, it did not reassure one sufficiently that the crown did actually intend to consult the estates on matters of importance to the nation. Barbat du Closel, therefore, placed at the disposal of the crown a *projet* of his own design. His plan called for the election of judges by the local estates for fixed terms; the establishment of a three-tiered court system—consisting of parlements (one in each généralité), sénéchaussées, and *bailliages royaux*—in which every company would be distinct in membership from every other one; and the firm guarantee that the *cour plenière* would function as a "national council" only in the intervals between meetings of the Estates-General.[39]

The last part of Barbat du Closel's program shows that still another result of the Maupeou years was that Frenchmen sharpened their focus on the kind of institutions needed to insure their participation in government. Bernardi, too, had been concerned that "the elite of the nation" be allowed the opportunity to deliberate with the crown in the making of laws. "The few good laws that we have," he said, "were made on the complaints of the Estates-General."[40]

Down to the time of Maupeou it had been possible to make the case that the parlements provided a not altogether inadequate substitute for the estates in this deliberative function. Montesquieu had called the parlements "le dépôt des lois." In fulfilling their role of "announcing the laws when they are made and recalling them when they are forgot," he had said, the parlements distinguished the French monarchy from despotism.[41] After the crown had shown, however, that it could suppress the parlements at will, few Frenchmen saw them as more than weak substitutes for some more secure deliberative body. Whereas in the sixteenth century Seyssel had expected the parlements to serve merely as a restraint or check (*frein*) on the crown, Diderot, in the 1770s, would have had the parlements be "a dam [*digue*] against the sovereign authority," "a barrier [*barrière*] thrown up for the defense of the people against . . . arbitrary power."[42] And clearly they were not doing so well in this larger role. The American Revolution, according to Linguet, only awakened in Frenchmen an even more exaggerated fear of despotism, which the old parlements were all the more incapable of allaying.[43]

If from a practical standpoint the parlements were incapable of keeping France from despotism, from a philosophical one they were even more unsatisfactory. The physiocrats had come to see the proper function of the courts as "prevent[ing] error from creeping into the Legislator's interpretation of the natural law."[44] The parlements tried to present themselves as the guardians of "les droits naturels" as well as of "les lois fondamentales." Judged unsatisfactory in both roles, they were held to be especially so in the new one.[45] First of all, as traditional corporations, they lost their legitimacy through the new theory of associations developed in the very natural law that they said they defended.[46] And second, they used what weapons they had—most notably, their right of remonstrance—very often to block reforms, particularly fiscal ones, desired by those of physiocratic sympathies. The "esprit de corps" shown by the parle-

9. *Les derniers efforts du Parlement auprès de la Justice* (*1790*). Anonymous.

ments completely vitiated whatever high-sounding claims they made.

Judicial reform thus became synonymous with constitutional change, and it was the desire for the latter which gave the final impetus to the judicial reforms of the Constituent Assembly. The momentum of legal reform throughout Europe, the sheer strain on French courts caused by growing population and social change, the increase of trade and the resulting need for regularity in justice, the notion that one was living in a "gentler," a more "civilized" age, in which the old institutions were no longer appropriate, and the recognition that royal attempts at reform had failed all made it inevitable that the courts would be a topic of concern to the Revolutionary legislators. The reforms that they would make, however, were very much the result of a long, indigenous, primarily intellectual development, the clarification of the modern concept of legislation.

# Conclusion

> History is like the Nile: one
> has gone up as far as the
> cataracts, but the true sources
> are well beyond.
>
> J.-M.-A. Servan

Although the source of the White Nile is now known, the metaphor will still serve. For it was composed at a time when the source of the river was not known, and when it did not seem likely that the source would be discovered at any time soon. Perhaps it is much the same with the reasons for the changes in programs for reform described in this work. One has penetrated as far as the influence of the modern idea of reform on legislation, but men's admission of that influence may have been only a symptom of deeper changes in the structure of their minds, caused by developments still more remote. Some distance has been covered, though, and perhaps one has indeed followed a stream going in the right direction.

The modern reforming tendencies of the Revolutionary legislators came to the fore very quickly. The cahiers de doléances had given clear indications of what might be done; if they had not, by and large, actually urged that the old courts be abolished, they had advocated so many, and such fundamental, changes in them as to imply their abolition.[1] In the first report on the judiciary done for the Constituent Assembly, Nicolas Bergasse, its author, set forth the principles of "le pouvoir judiciaire"; none were fulfilled by the old courts, which, in his mind, had been set up to do something altogether different than "serve the general will."[2] "Our magistrature," he said, "was strongly instituted in order to resist despotism; but now that there is no more despotism, if our magistrature conserved all the strength of its foundation, the employment of this force could easily become dangerous to liberty. It is then indispensable that a complete revolution take place in the system of our courts.[3] Bergasse wrote this report extremely fast. According to one historian, "the rapidity with which Bergasse was able to treat such a vast subject shows that the essential ideas about the subject belonged already to the public domain."[4] If there could be any doubt that a complete reform of the courts was expected from the start, the fact that the assembly voted down a resolution in March 1790 to extend for a mere three days the debate over whether there should be such a reform would surely put it to rest. Even the defenders of the parlements made a feeble case for them. De Cazalès could only say that it was "to the general patriotism of the parlements" that the legislators "owed the Estates-General, and hence the National Assembly."[5] A major argument of an anonymous writer of 1790 was that abolishing the parlements was not consistent with the aims of a government seeking to "economize."[6]

The debate over exactly what should take the place of the old courts was much fuller. The questions of whether judges should be sedentary or ambulatory, of whether there should be juries (and if so, whether they should be instituted for civil as well as criminal cases), and of whether the people should elect judges or the king (or legislative power) should appoint them all exercised the minds of the Revolutionaries for many, many hours.[7] The most impressive and influential speeches were those of Jacques-Guillaume Thouret, the avocat from Normandy who would be guillotined in April 1794, but innumerable others were also delivered, many of which were, in addition, printed and distributed. The English theoretician Jeremy Bentham even sent in his ideas for the assembly to consider.[8]

An occasional note of consternation was heard as the work of the assembly proceeded, as when Prugnon observed, in May 1790, "Locke, d'Aguesseau, Montesquieu, and L'Hospital, if they were on your Comité de constitution and one wanted them to reform everything, would quickly hand in their resignations."[9] Démeunier saved the commercial courts, which were in danger of becoming victims of the campaign to eliminate all exceptional jurisdictions, by citing the number of cases that they had tried during the previous year (80,000 in Paris; 16,000 in Bordeaux) and convincingly arguing that the ordinary courts could never pick up such a case load.[10] But in general, the actions as well as the intentions of the revolutionaries with respect to the judiciary, as to so many other institutions of old France, were consistent with this theme from one of Thouret's addresses: "The necessity of the absolute regeneration is incontestable. Not only will the constitution be incomplete if it does not embrace all the parts that should essentially compose it, but also will it be vicious, incoherent, and unstable if all these parts are not harmonized."[11]

An interesting side light is that the principle of the présidial jurisdiction was rejected because it was found to be inconsistent with the new principle of equality. A small suit, said Duport, was just as important to a poor man as a large suit was to a rich man, hence why, he asked, should the one be subject to final judgment in an intermediary court and the other be permitted to reach the highest courts?[12] Some decades before the Revolution, Linguet had expressed the nearly opposite concern that small artisans' claims were being excluded from the expeditious justice of the présidiaux because they were slightly too big. He had urged that the présidiaux be given a greater competence to protect the less prosperous litigants from the financial ruin attendant upon being dragged through lengthy proceedings and taken all the way to the parlements.[13] So complete was the revolutionaries' attachment to, and so rigorous was their application of, the principles that guided them that they could not depart from them even when they stood in danger of violating them.

In the introduction to this book, I illustrated the distinction between traditional and modern reform by using the metaphor of different approaches to correcting the bent tine of a fork. It then occurred to me to look into the history of the fork and see just what was being done in the seventeenth and eighteenth centuries to insure the adequacy of tableware. What I found, sure enough, was that the period saw the beginnings of the redesigning of knives and forks that would culminate in the early nineteenth century with silverware precisely suited to its particular function. As early as the seventeenth century a *couteau à patisserie* made its appearance; by the nineteenth the smiths and manufacturers had supplied the bourgeois household with the *couvert à salade*, the *service à poisson*, and *fourchettes à huitres, à escargots, à viande froide, à dessert, à melon,* and *de cuisine,* as well as with *services à découper* in the styles of the Empire, Louis-Philippe, and the Third Republic.[14] The influence of modern reformism had been so broad as to affect even common craftsmen in their work and so deep as to change the preferences of the middle classes even with respect to such mundane matters as the design of their eating utensils.

The reader will remember that L'Hospital urged that there be different courts for different kinds of cases. The functionalism of the

*Labrousse del. et Sculp.*                           *J.<sup></sup> Sauveur direx.*

*Membre du Tribunal de Cassation.*

10. *Membre du Tribunal de cassation* (*New Costume Proposal, 1795*), by L. Labrousse.

sixteenth-century chancellor was that of Roman law, however, rather than that of Cartesianism. If not merely nominal, it was rudimentary; and it was still enmeshed with innumerable social distinctions whereby cases of the same kind involving people of different orders or corporate groups went, according to no explicable rule, to separate courts. Modern reformers judged that the courts of the Old Regime were inadequately, even falsely differentiated, that the divisions between them did not proceed from principles of sufficient consistency, clarity, and validity, that their functionalism was of an outmoded type, that they showed no more sophistication or promise, indeed, in their structure and organization than the results of the slow and groping attempts in the sixteenth century to design the first serviceable forks. Frenchmen of the late eighteenth century surely admired in many respects the efforts of the traditional reformers, but they believed themselves capable of much better. For they had learned a method.

# Notes

## Introduction

1. Emile Littré, *Dictionnaire de la langue française* (Paris, 1881–1883), IV, 1546; Jean Dubois, *Lexis: Dictionnaire de la langue française* (Paris: Larousse, 1975), pp. 1512–1513.

2. William Smith and Theophilus D. Hall, *A Copious and Critical English-Latin Dictionary* (New York, 1871), p. 658.

3. René Descartes, *Oeuvres philosophiques*, ed. Ferdinand Alquié (Paris: Garnier, 1963–1973), I, 582, 586 (*Discours de la méthode pour bien conduire sa raison et chercher la vérité dans les sciences*, Part II, §14–15, 18).

4. Ibid., p. 582 (*Discours de la méthode*, Part II, §14–15).

5. Henri-François d'Aguesseau, *Lettres inédites du chancelier d'Aguesseau*, ed. D. B. Rives (Paris, 1823), I, 132.

6. René-Nicolas-Charles-Augustin de Maupeou, "Mémoire de Maupeou à Louis XVI" (1789), as reproduced in the appendix to Jules Flammermont, *Le Chancelier Maupeou et les parlements* (Paris, 1883), p. 622.

7. Pierre Victor, baron de Besenval, *Mémoires de M. le baron de Besenval*, ed. Alexandre-Joseph Pierre, vicomte de Ségur (Paris, 1805–1807), III, 4–6.

8. Henri-François d'Aguesseau, "Mémoire sur les vues générales que l'on peut avoir pour la réformation de la justice" (1725), in *Oeuvres complètes du chancelier d'Aguesseau*, ed. Jean-Marie Pardessus (Paris, 1819), XIII, 200–229.

9. Henri-François d'Aguesseau, *Mémoire inédit du chancelier Daguesseau sur la réformation de la justice*, ed. Paule Combe (Valence: Imprimés réunies, 1928), pp. 133–136.

## 1. Judicial Reform in the Sixteenth and Seventeenth Centuries

1. Numa Denis Fustel de Coulanges, "La justice en France sous la monarchie absolue," *Revue des deux mondes*, 95 (1871), 570–601; Frédéric Cheyette, "La justice et le pouvoir royal à la fin du Moyen Age français," *Revue historique de droit français et étranger*, 4th ser., 40 (1962), 373–394.

2. Niccolò Machiavelli, "Tableau des choses de la France" (1510), in *Toutes les lettres officielles et familières, celles de ses seigneurs, de ses amis et des siens*, ed. Edmond Barincou (Paris: Gallimard, 1955), II, 252–261; Niccolò Machiavelli, *The Prince and The Discourses*, trans. Luigi Ricci and Christian E. Detmold (New York: Random House, 1950), p. 69 (*The Prince* [written 1513; published 1532], chap. XIX).

3. Machiavelli, *The Prince and The Discourses*, trans. Ricci and Detmold, pp. 401–402 (*Discourses on the First Ten Books of Titus Livius* [written ca. 1513–1519; published 1531], Third Book, chap. I).

4. Claude de Seyssel, *La monarchie de France et deux autres fragments politiques*, ed. Jacques Poujol (Paris: Librairie d'Argences, 1961), p. 117.

5. Marcel Marion, *Dictionnaire des institutions de la France aux XVIIᵉ et XVIIIᵉ*

*siècles* (1923; reprint ed., Paris: Picard, 1968), pp. 204, 480–481; Jean H. Mariéjol, *La Réforme et la Ligue: L'Edit de Nantes (1559–1598)*, in Ernest Lavisse, ed., *Histoire de France depuis les origines jusqu'à la Révolution* (Paris: Hachette, 1903–1911), VI, Part I, p. 86.

6. Philippe de Commynes, *Mémoires,* ed. Joseph Calmette (Paris: H. Champion, 1924–1925), I, 164 (Book II, chap. XIV: "La Destruction de Liège").

7. François Hotman, *Francogallia,* ed. and trans. Ralph E. Giesey and J. H. M. Salmon (Cambridge, Eng.: Cambridge University Press, 1972), pp. 497, 503, 505 (chap. XX: "The Parlements as Courts of Law").

8. Guy Coquille, *Dialogue sur les causes des misères de la France, entre un Catholique Ancien, un Catholique Zélé, et un Palatin* (1590), in *Les oeuvres de Maistre Guy de Coquille, Sieur de Romenay, contenant plusieurs traitez touchant les libertez de l'Eglise gallicane, l'histoire de France et le droit françois,* ed. Claude Labottiere (Bordeaux, 1703), I, 215.

9. François Marie Arouet de Voltaire, "L'équivoque" (1771), *Oeuvres complètes de Voltaire,* ed. Louis Morland (Paris, 1877–1885), XXVIII, 422.

10. Michel L'Hospital, "Harangue à l'ouverture du Parlement de Paris" (November 12, 1563), *Oeuvres complètes de Michel L'Hospital, chancelier de France,* ed. P. J. S. Duféy (Paris, 1824–1825), II, 92, 95–96.

11. Michel de Marillac, "Mémoire dressé principalement contre l'autorité du Parlement," n.d., ms. 825, Bibliothèque Sainte-Geneviève.

12. Franklin L. Ford, *Robe and Sword: The Regrouping of the French Aristocracy after Louis XIV* (Cambridge, Mass.: Harvard University Press, 1953), pp. 121–123.

13. Julian H. Franklin, *Jean Bodin and the Rise of Absolutist Theory* (Cambridge, Eng.: Cambridge University Press, 1973), pp. 4–5.

14. Charles Loyseau, *Les Cinq Livres du Droit des Offices* (1610), in *Les oeuvres de Maistre Charles Loyseau, avocat en parlement: Contenant les Cinq Livres du Droit des Offices, les Traitez des Seigneuries, des Ordres et simples Dignitez, du Déguerpissement et Délaissement par Hypothèque de la Garantie des Rentes, et des Abus des Justices de Villages* (Paris, 1678), p. 156 (each work is paginated separately).

15. Ennamond Dominique Nicolas Fayard, *Aperçu historique sur le Parlement de Paris* (Lyon and Paris, 1876–1878), I, 213–214.

16. Jean Racine, *Les plaideurs* (1669), in *Théâtre de Racine,* ed. Pierre Mélèse (Paris: Imprimerie nationale de France, 1951), II, 146–147 (act I, sc. 7).

17. Ange Cappel, *L'advis donne au roy sur l'abréviation des procès* (1562; reprint ed., Paris? ca. 1600), p. 53.

18. Jean Bodin, *The Six Bookes of a Commonweale,* trans. Richard Knolles (1606); ed. Kenneth Douglas McRae (Cambridge, Mass.: Harvard University Press, 1962), pp. 766–767 (Book VI, chap. 6). Based on Bodin's French original of 1576 and his Latin version completed in 1584 and published in 1586.

19. Jean Domat, "Harangue prononcée aux assises de 1671," *Oeuvres complètes de Jean Domat,* ed. Joseph Rémy (Paris, 1828–1830), IV, 50.

20. As quoted by Charles Bataillard, "Tableau des principaux abus existant dans le monde judiciaire au XVI$^e$ siècle," *Mémoires de la Société impériale des antiquaires de France* (Paris), 23 (1857), 213–214.

21. Fernand Braudel, *The Mediterranean and the Mediterranean World in the Age of Philip II,* trans. Siân Reynolds (New York: Harper & Row, 1973; French orig. 1949), II, 734–756.

22. Marc Bloch, *French Rural History: An Essay on Its Basic Characteristics,* trans. Janet Sondheimer (Berkeley, Calif.: University of California Press, 1966; French orig. 1931), pp. 128–135.

23. Guy Coquille, "Discours sur les maux presens du royaume (pièce non achevée)" (ca. 1590), *Les oeuvres de Maistre Guy de Coquille,* ed. Labottiere (1703), I, 240–242.

24. François Rabelais, *The Histories of Gargantua and Pantagruel,* trans. J. M. Cohen (Baltimore: Penguin Books, 1955), pp. 625–636 (Book V, chaps. 11–15). The French original is in François Rabelais, *Oeuvres complètes,* ed. Pierre Jourda (Paris: Garnier, 1962), II, 316–332. Book V was published in 1564, after Rabelais' death, and some consider it spurious.

25. Michel L'Hospital. "Traité de la réformation de la justice," *Oeuvres inédites de Michel L'Hospital, chancelier de France,* ed. P. J. S. Duféy (Paris, 1825–1826), I, 67–68. The "Traité" remained unpublished at L'Hospital's death in 1573. Unfortunately, some parts of the manuscript can have been written no earlier than the seventeenth century. As Duféy notes in the preface to his edition, the apparent interpolations are conspicuous for their anachronistic style and content. Their extent, however, suggests caution about the rest of the work as well.

26. Rabelais, *Gargantua and Pantagruel,* trans. Cohen (1955), p. 628 (Book V, chap. 11); in Rabelais, *Oeuvres complètes,* ed. Jourda (1962), II, 320. This passage was called to my attention by Donald M. Frame, *François Rabelais: A Study* (New York: Harcourt Brace Jovanovich, 1977), pp. 92–94, where it is also cited and discussed.

27. Armand Jean du Plessis, Cardinal de Richelieu, *Testament politique,* ed. Louis André (Paris: R. Laffont, 1947), pp. 235–236 (Part I, chap. 4, sect. 1). Thought to be based on a manuscript discovered after the cardinal's death in 1642. First published in 1688.

28. Roger Doucet, *Les institutions de la France au XVIᵉ siècle* (Paris: Picard, 1948), I, 406–419.

29. Jean Savaron, *Traicté de l'annuel et venalité des offices* (Paris, 1615), p. 14.

30. Coquille, "Que les maux de la France pendant la Ligue venoit faute de reformation, principalement de l'Etat Ecclesiastique" (ca. 1590), *Les oeuvres de Maistre Guy de Coquille,* ed. Labottiere (1703), I, 265.

31. Bodin, *Six Bookes of a Commonweale,* ed. McRae (1962), pp. 591–592 (Book V, chap. 4).

32. Ibid., p. 789 (Book VI, chap. 6).

33. L'Hospital, "Traité," *Oeuvres inédites,* ed. Duféy (1825–1826), II, 121.

34. Lancelot Voysin, sieur de La Popelinière, *L'histoire de France enrichie des plus notables occurrances survenues ez provinces de l'Europe et pays voisins, soit en paix soit en guerre: tant pour le fait seculier qu'eclesiastic: depuis lan 1550 jusques a ces temps* (La Rochelle, 1581), I, fol. 230.

35. Jonathon Dewald, *The Magistrates of the Parlement of Rouen, 1499–1610* (Ann Arbor: University Microfilms, 1974), pp. 44–46.

36. Coquille, *Dialogue sur les causes des misères de la France* (1590), *Les oeuvres de Maistre Guy de Coquille,* ed. Labottiere (1703), I, 233.

37. L'Hospital, "Traité," *Oeuvres inédites,* ed. Duféy (1825–1826), II, 118.

38. Roland Mousnier, *La vénalité des offices sous Henri IV et Louis XIII,* 2nd ed. (Paris: Presses universitaires de France, 1971), pp. 72–77, 356–369, 455–528.

39. Ford, *Robe and Sword,* pp. 148–155.

40. Julian Dent, *Crisis in Finance: Crown, Finances and Society in Seventeenth-Century France* (Newton Abbot, Eng.: David & Charles, 1973), pp. 57–61.

41. Mousnier, *La vénalité des offices,* 2nd ed. (1971), pp. 7–8.

42. Michel Eyquem, seigneur de Montaigne, *The Complete Essays of Montaigne,* trans. Donald M. Frame (Stanford, Calif.: Stanford University Press, 1958), pp.

86, 88 (Book I, chap. 23: "Of custom, and not easily changing an accepted law").
Fr. orig. contained in Michel Eyquem, seigneur de Montaigne, *Essais,* ed.
Maurice Rat (Paris: Garnier, 1962), I, 125, 128. The first edition of the *Essais*
(1580) contained Books I and II only.

43. Jean de la Bruyère, *Characters,* trans. Jean Stewart (Baltimore: Penguin
Books, 1970), pp. 166–167 (Chap. X, part 7: "Of the Sovereign, and the State").
Fr. orig. contained in Jean de La Bruyère, *Les caractères de Théophraste traduits du
grec avec Les caractères ou les moeurs de ce siècle,* ed. Robert Garapon (Paris: Garnier,
1962), pp. 276–277. La Bruyère's work obtained the royal privilege in 1687 and
was first sold in 1688.

44. L'Hospital, "Traité," *Oeuvres inédites,* ed. Duféy (1825–1826), II, 14.

45. Bodin, *Six Bookes of a Commonweale,* ed. McRae (1962), pp. 467–475 (Book
IV, chap. 3).

46. Richelieu, *Testament politique,* ed. André (1947), p. 234 (Part I, chap. 4,
section 1).

47. One must say "perhaps" because the proposal may have been that of
L'Hospital's seventeenth-century editor.

48. Cappel, *L'advis donne au roy* (1562; reprint ed., ca. 1600), pp. 50–57, 62–63.

49. Philibert Bonet, *Moyens pour abreger les procès et oster les empeschemens de bonne
et brefve expedition de iustice* (Paris, 1556), pp. 11–16.

50. François Du Noyer, *Articles, que presente au roy François du Noyer sieur de S.
Martin, pour establir une compagnie, afin de rendre la iustice gratuitement en France, et regler
les benefices, oster la venalité des offices et charges. Avec les moyens pour y parvenir approuvez
par les Estats Generaux n'agueres tenus en la ville de Paris* (Paris, 1616), p. 36.

51. Denis Diderot, *Mémoires pour Cathérine II,* ed. Paul Vernière (Paris: Garnier, 1966), p. 45 (Book III: "De l'administration de la justice"; written in 1773).

52. *Le labyrinthe de l'estat, ou les veritables causes des malheurs de la France. A Ctesiphon* (Paris, 1652), pp. 12–13.

53. Marion, *Dictionnaire des institutions,* pp. 453–454.

54. For text of Ordonnance of Villers-Cotterêts, see François André Isambert
et al., eds., *Recueil général des anciennes lois françaises, depuis l'an 420 jusqu'à la Révolution de 1789* (Paris, 1821–1833), XII, 600–640.

55. J. Michael Hayden, *France and the Estates General of 1614* (London: Cambridge University Press, 1974), p. 186, n. 20.

56. Ernest Laurain, *Essai sur les présidiaux* (Paris, 1896), p. 23

57. Coquille, "Mémoire de ce qui est à faire pour le bien du pays de Nivernois, envoyé à Monsieur de Nevers, par Maître Erard Bardin, qui est party le 18.
Août 1573," *Les oeuvres de Maistre Guy de Coquille,* ed. Labottiere (1703), I, 260, 269.

58. Coquille, "Qu'en fait d'estats les gouvernemens, les bailliages et senê-
chaussées ne doivent être en consideration, et encores moins les sieges présidiaux"
(ca. 1591), *Les oeuvres de Maistre Guy de Coquille,* ed. Labottiere (1703), I, 287.

59. Paul Garcin, "Michel de L'Hospital et les tribunaux consulaires," *Revue
des deux mondes,* n.s., 16 (1963), 118–125.

60. Bataillard, "Tableau des principaux abus," pp. 199–200.

61. Marion, *Dictionnaire des institutions,* pp. 139–140.

62. L'Hospital, "Traité," *Oeuvres inédites,* ed. Duféy (1825–1826), II, 191–
193, 247.

63. Ibid., pp. 146–147, 248–249.

64. Ibid., I, 348–368.

65. Du Noyer, *Articles, que presente au roy François du Noyer* (1616), p. 3. Following citations from pp. 3–9, 20–21, 24–34, 36–38, 47, 49–53, 56.

66. Marc Chassaigne, "Un manuel de procédure criminelle au XVIᵉ siècle," *Revue des études historiques*, 79 (1913), 294–317, 402–437.

67. Bodin, *Six Bookes of a Commonweale*, ed. McRae (1962), pp. 783–784 (Book VI, chap. 6).

68. See Jean Marquiset, *Les gens de justice dans la littérature* (Paris: Librairie Générale de Droit et de Jurisprudence, 1967), pp. 163–186.

69. Adam Smith, *An Inquiry into the Nature and Causes of the Wealth of Nations* (1776), ed. Edward Gibbon Wakefield (London, 1843), IV, 45 (Book V, chap. 1, part 2).

70. Ernest H. Kossmann, *La Fronde* (Leiden: Universitaire Pers Leiden, 1954), pp. 25–26.

71. Ford, *Robe and Sword;* Jean Meyer, *La noblesse bretonne au XVIIIᵉ siècle* (Paris: Flammarion, 1972).

72. Albert Dauzat, Jean Dubois, and Henri Mitterand, *Nouveau dictionnaire étymologique et historique* (Paris: Larousse, 1971), p. 31.

73. Charles de Figon, *Discours des estats et offices, tant du gouvernement que de la justice et des finances de France* (Paris, 1608), from the dedication (not paginated).

74. Ibid., p. 7.

75. L'Hospital, "Traité," *Oeuvres inédites,* ed. Duféy (1825–1826), I, 285–288.

76. Diana C. T. Flamholtz, *Etienne Pasquier and the High Magistracy during the French Wars of Religion* (Ann Arbor: University Microfilms, 1972), pp. 40–48.

77. J. H. M. Salmon, *Society in Crisis: France in the Sixteenth Century* (London: E. Benn, 1975), p. 157.

78. Bodin, *Six Bookes of a Commonweale*, ed. McRae (1962), p. 108 (Book I, chap. 8).

79. Bonet, *Moyens pour abreger les procès* (1556), p. 20.

80. Ibid., pp. 32–34.

81. Seyssel, *La monarchie de France,* ed. Poujol (1961), pp. 149–150.

82. [Antoine Loisel], *De l'oeil des rois et de la iustice. Remonstrance faite en la ville de Bordeaux à l'ouverture de la cour de iustice envoyée par le roy en ses païs et Duché de Guienne* (Paris, 1584), pp. xvii–xviii.

83. L'Hospital, "Traité," *Oeuvres inédites,* ed. Duféy (1825–1826), II, 142.

84. Bonet, *Moyens pour abreger les procès* (1556), pp. 14, 21.

85. Aristotle, *Problems II: Rhetorica ad Alexandrum,* trans., W. S. Hett and H. Rackham, Loeb Classical Library (1937; reprint ed., Cambridge, Mass.: Harvard University Press, 1965), pp. 277–279 (*Treatise on Rhetoric Dedicated to Alexander,* Book I).

86. Domat, "Harangue prononcée aux assises de l'année 1672," *Oeuvres complètes,* ed. Rémy (1828–1830), IV, 53.

87. See Barry Nicholas, *An Introduction to Roman Law* (Oxford: Oxford University Press, 1962), pp. 45–51; and Wolfgang Kunkel, *An Introduction to Roman Legal and Constitutional History,* 2nd ed., trans. J. M. Kelly (Oxford: Oxford University Press, 1973; based on 6th German ed.), pp. 163–191.

88. Seyssel, *La monarchie de France,* ed. Poujol (1961), pp. 127, 149–154.

89. L'Hospital, "Traité," *Oeuvres inédites,* ed. Duféy (1825–1826), I, 27.

90. L'Hospital, "Au Roi Charles IX et à la Reine-Mère: Fragment d'un mémoire adressé à Charles IX et à la Reine-Mère, après la première retraite du chancelier L'Hospital" (1562), *Oeuvres complétes,* ed. Duféy (1824–1825), II, 254.

91. L'Hospital, "Traité," *Oeuvres inédites,* ed. Duféy (1825–1826), I, 28.

92. Ibid., p. 82.

93. Ibid., p. 76.

94. Ibid., p. 111.

95. Jean de Coras, *Discours des parties et office d'un bon et entier juge* (1559; reprint ed., Lyon, [1618]), p. 37.

96. Mical H. Schneider, *The French Magistracy*, 1560–1615 (Ann Arbor: University Microfilms, 1974), p. 248.

97. Jacques Labitte, *Règlement pour la réformation et abbréviation de la iustice du Duché de Mayne et sieges qui en dépendent* (Paris, 1582).

98. Coquille, "Mémoire de ce qui est à faire pour le bien du pays de Nivernois ... 1573," *Les oeuvres de Maistre Guy de Coquille*, ed. Labottiere (1703), I, 269.

99. Claude Collot, *L'école doctrinale de droit public de Pont-à-Mousson: Pierre Grégoire de Toulouse et Guillaume Barclay, fin du XVI\* siècle* (Paris: Librairie Générale de Droit et de Jurisprudence, 1965), pp. 188–189.

100. Loyseau, *Discours de l'abus des justices de village* (1603–1604), *Les oeuvres de Maistre Charles Loyseau* (ed. 1678), pp. 13–14.

101. Bodin, *Six Bookes of a Commonweale*, ed. McRae (1962), p. 113 (Book I, chap. 8).

102. Ibid., p. 755 (Book VI, chap. 6).

103. Ibid., p. 761 (Book VI, chap. 6).

104. Ibid., pp. 784–790 (Book VI, chap. 6).

105. Ibid., pp. 218–230 (Book II, chap. 5: "Whether it be lawfull to lay violent hand upon a tyrant; and after his death to disannul all his acts, decrees, and lawes"). See also pp. 632–633 (Book V, chap. 6).

106. Charles Loyseau, *Traité des seigneuries* (Paris, 1608), from the dedication (not paginated).

107. Jean Domat, *Les loix civiles dans leur ordre naturel*, 2nd ed. (Paris, 1696–1697), I, preface (not paginated).

108. Bernard le Bovier de Fontenelle, "Préface sur l'utilité des mathématiques et de la physique, et sur les travaux de l'Académie des Sciences" (1702), *Oeuvres de Fontenelle*, ed. G. B. Depping (Paris, 1818), I, 34.

109. D'Aguesseau, *Oeuvres complètes*, ed. Pardessus (1819), XV, 114.

110. Another sixteenth-century jurist who would have worked great organizational changes in the courts was Raoul Spifame, who proposed a set of 306 reforming laws to Henry II in 1556, of which 119 concerned the judiciary. See Yves Jeanclos, *Les projets de réforme judiciaire de Raoul Spifame au XVI\* siècle* (Geneva: Droz, 1977).

111. On Colbert and his legal and judicial reforms see: Pierre Clément, *Histoire de Colbert et de son administration* (Paris, 1874), II, 291–362; and Mary Jane Parrine, *Legal Reformism and Codification under Louis XIV: The Sense of Criminal Justice* (Ann Arbor: University Microfilms, 1974). Parrine notes that Colbert's commissions marked the first time that a large group of royal officials and other experts had met to discuss reform systematically in order to make recommendations to the crown. Previous reforms, like the omnibus, diffuse reform ordonnances of the fifteenth, sixteenth, and early seventeenth centuries, had been composed and enacted upon the recommendations of the Estates-General.

112. Reprinted in Guy Thuillier, "Economie et administration au grand siècle: L'Abbé Claude Fleury," *La revue administrative*, 10 (1957), 353–354.

113. Domat, *Le droit public, suite des loix civiles dans leur ordre naturel* (1697), Book IV, *Oeuvres complètes*, ed. Rémy (1828–1830), III, 573.

114. Guy Thuillier, "Une 'utopie' au grand siècle: 'De la Réformation d'un

Etat' de Géraud de Cordemoy (1668)," *La revue administrative,* 13 (1960), 257–262.
115. S. V. Keeling, *Descartes,* 2nd ed. (Oxford: Oxford University Press, 1968), pp. 192, n. 1, 213, 232, n. 1.

## 2. Objectives of Judicial Reform in the Eighteenth Century

1. Charles-Irénée Castel, l'abbé de Saint-Pierre, *Mémoire pour diminuer le nombre des procès* (1715; 2nd ed. Paris, 1725), pp. Ai(r)–Aii.
2. Charles-Irénée Castel, l'abbé de Saint-Pierre, *Ouvrajes* [*sic*] *de politique* (Rotterdam, 1733–1741), VII, 78–79.
3. Saint-Pierre, *Mémoire pour diminuer le nombre des procès* (1725), pp. Aii, 8–9, 27, 93–94.
4. Ibid., pp. 92, 98–100.
5. This last motivation of Saint-Pierre to advocate judicial reform is suggested in Merle L. Perkins, *The Moral and Political Philosophy of the Abbé de Saint-Pierre* (Geneva: Droz, 1959), p. 104.
6. Saint-Pierre, *Mémoire pour diminuer le nombre des procès* (1725), pp. 104–105.
7. Ibid., pp. 94–103.
8. Ibid., pp. 280–281.
9. Bodin, *Six Bookes of a Commonweale,* ed. McRae (1962), pp. 766–767 (Book VI, chap. 6).
10. Saint-Pierre, *Mémoire pour diminuer le nombre des procès* (1725), pp. 30–31, 52–53, 94.
11. Henri-François d'Aguesseau, "Mémoires sur la réforme de la législation: Premier mémoire," reproduced in appendix to Francis Monnier, *Le Chancelier d'Aguesseau: Sa conduite et ses idées politiques et son influence sur le mouvement des esprits pendant la première moitié du XVIII⁰ siècle* (Paris, 1860), p. 459.
12. Saint-Pierre, *Mémoire pour diminuer le nombre des procès* (1725), pp. 36–37, 64–65.
13. René-Louis de Voyer, marquis d'Argenson, *Journal et mémoires du marquis d'Argenson,* ed. Edme Jacques Benoît Rathéry (Paris, 1859–1867), II, 19.
14. René-Louis de Voyer, marquis d'Argenson, *Mémoires et journal inédit du marquis d'Argenson, ministre des affaires étrangères sous Louis XV,* ed. Charles Marc René de Voyer, marquis d'Argenson (Paris, 1857–1858), V, 259–260. For a discussion of the two editions of d'Argenson's memoirs, see: Nannerl Overholsen Henry, *Democratic Monarchy: The Political Thought of the Marquis d'Argenson* (Ann Arbor: University Microfilms, 1968), pp. 303–307. Briefly, the editions are in general agreement, but each has its shortcomings. Rathéry reproduced d'Argenson's jolting style, while the marquis' descendant polished it. But the descendant had access to family papers that Rathéry did not, and so his edition is richer in places. Most of d'Argenson's manuscripts were destroyed shortly after these two editions appeared, in the Louvre fire of 1871.
15. D'Aguesseau, "Mémoire sur les vues générales que l'on peut avoir pour la réformation de la justice," *Oeuvres complètes,* ed. Pardessus (1819), XIII, 200–229.
16. Ibid., p. 215.
17. Ibid.
18. D'Aguesseau, *Mémoire inédit sur la réformation de la justice,* ed. Combe (1928), p. 138.
19. D'Aguesseau, *Oeuvres complètes,* ed. Pardessus (1819), XV, 21.
20. D'Aguesseau, "Mémoire sur les vues générales pour la réformation de la justice," *Oeuvres complètes,* ed. Pardessus (1819), XIII, 200–202.
21. D'Aguesseau, *Oeuvres complètes,* ed. Pardessus (1819), XVI, 228–229.

22. D'Aguesseau, "Mémoire sur les vues générales pour la réformation de la justice," *Oeuvres complètes,* ed. Pardessus (1819), XIII, 216–217, 224–226.

23. Ibid., pp. 227, 229.

24. D'Aguesseau to La Briffe, Intendant of Burgundy, January 25, 1740. A.D. de la Côte-d'Or, C. 4.

25. D'Aguesseau, *Mémoire inédit sur la réformation de la justice,* ed. Combe (1928), p. 145.

26. Ibid.

27. Compare John Philip Dawson, "The Judges in the Bailliages and Sénéchaussées, 1763–1800: A Study of Middle-Class Office-Holders before and during the French Revolution" (Ph.D. thesis, Harvard University, 1961), pp. 93–98. Here it would be stressed more that d'Aguesseau was less timid in conception than in execution.

28. In introducing d'Aguesseau's *Mémoire inédit sur la réformation de la justice,* Combe stated that the chancellor only once actually suggested that the parlements needed reform and that on this occasion he thought the parlements principally needed scaling down. "There are today nearly as many officers in the single Parlement of Paris," Combe quoted him as saying, "as there were in the eight parlements of the realm that existed at the time of the Ordonnance of Blois." (p. 87)

29. Dawson, "The Judges in the Bailliages and Sénéchaussées," p. 78.

30. D'Aguesseau, *Oeuvres complètes,* ed. Pardessus (1819), XI, 110; XII, 180–184.

31. See John Law, *Oeuvres complètes,* ed. Paul Harsin (Paris: Librairie du Recueil Sirey, 1934), II, 202, 305.

32. J. Balteau et al., *Dictionnaire de biographie française* (Paris: Letouzey, 1933–   ), I, 830.

33. D'Aguesseau, "Mémoire sur les vues générales pour la réformation de la justice," *Oeuvres complètes,* ed. Pardessus (1819), XIII, 217.

34. Ibid., p. 217.

35. Barthélemy-Joseph Bretonnier, *Recueil par ordre alphabétique des principales questions de droit, qui se jugent diversement dans les différens tribunaux du royaume. Avec des réflexions pour concilier la diversité de la jurisprudence, et la rendre uniforme dans tous les tribunaux,* 3rd ed. (Paris, 1752–1753; first ed. 1718), I, xcv–xcvi.

36. D'Argenson, *Mémoires et journal inédit,* ed. d'Argenson (1857–1858), I, 16.

37. Ibid., V, 259.

38. Ibid., p. 270.

39. René-Louis de Voyer, marquis d'Argenson, *Considérations sur le gouvernement ancien et présent de la France* (1764; 2nd ed. Amsterdam, 1765). D'Argenson apparently wrote this work as early as the 1730s.

40. Ibid., pp. 267–270.

41. Ibid., pp. 27–34, 215–218, 221–230.

42. Ibid., p. 221.

43. Ibid., p. 35.

44. D'Argenson, *Journal et mémoires,* ed. Rathéry (1859–1867), II, 19.

45. D'Argenson, *Considérations sur le gouvernement* (1765), pp. 16–17.

46. D'Argenson, *Mémoires et journal inédit,* ed. d'Argenson (1857–1858), V, 204–205.

47. D'Argenson, *Considérations sur le gouvernement* (1765), pp. 17–18.

48. D'Argenson, *Journal et mémoires,* ed. Rathéry (1859–1867), II, 19.

49. D'Argenson, *Considérations sur le gouvernement* (1765), p. 156.

50. Ibid., pp. 157–161.

51. Balteau et al., *Dictionnaire de biographie*, III, 558.

52. D'Argenson, *Mémoires et journal inédit*, ed. d'Argenson (1857–1858), V, 307. This passage was called to my attention by Henry, *Democratic Monarchy*, pp. 244–245, where it is also cited and discussed.

53. Joseph-Michel-Antoine Servan, *Discours sur le progrès des connoissances humaines en général, de la morale, et de la législation en particulier; lu dans une assemblée publique de l'Académie de Lyon* (n.p., 1781), pp. 38–39.

54. Henry, *Democratic Monarchy*, pp. 188–196.

55. Jean-Jacques Rousseau, *The Political Writings of Jean-Jacques Rousseau*, ed. C. E. Vaughan (1915; reprint ed., Oxford: Blackwell, 1962), II, 352–353, 472–475. Rousseau wrote his four *Lettres à M. Butta-Foco sur la législation de la Corse* in 1764–1765, and his *Considérations sur le gouvernement de Pologne* in 1771–1772.

*3. New Directions in Royal Programs for Court Reform*

1. Loyseau, *Les Cinq Livres du Droit des Offices* (1610), in *Les oeuvres de Maistre Charles Loyseau* (ed. 1678), p. 152.

2. See Theodore Zeldin, *France 1848–1945* (Oxford: Oxford University Press, 1973–1977), I, 113–130.

3. See Edouard Evérat, *La Sénéchaussée d'Auvergne et siège présidial de Riom au XVIII^e siècle* (Paris, 1885), pp. 50–65; Albert Macé, "La réforme des présidiaux au XVIII^e siècle," *Bulletin de la Société polymathique du Morbihan*, 36 (1890), 127–137; and Laurain, *Essai sur les présidiaux*, pp. 77–83.

4. Louis-Jean-Baptiste Bucquet, *Discours qui a remporté le prix à l'Académie de Chaalons, en l'année M.DCC.LXXXIII. Sur cette question proposée par la même académie: Quels seroient les moyens de rendre la justice en France avec le plus de célérité et le moins de frais possibles?* (Beauvais, 1789), pp. 103–104.

5. Bailliage of Châteaulin to Camus de Pontcarré de Viarme, Intendant of Brittany, June 4, 1740. A.D. d'Ille-et-Vilaine, C. 1835.

6. Maguelone de St. Benoit, judge in Présidial of Limoux, to Guignard de Saint-Priest, Intendant of Languedoc, October 13, 1766. A.D. de l'Hérault, C. 60.

7. "Mémoire présenté au roi par le Présidial de Nîmes réclamant la noblesse pour tous les officiers présidiaux du royaume," 1782. A.D. de la Drôme, B. 629.

8. Sénéchaussée of Guérande to Camus de Pontcarré de Viarme, Intendant of Brittany, August 21, 1740. A.D. d'Ille-et-Vilaine, C. 1835.

9. Présidial of Nantes to Camus de Pontcarré de Viarme, Intendant of Brittany, April 3, 1740. A.D. d'Ille-et-Vilaine, C. 1836.

10. Présidial of Vannes to Camus de Pontcarré de Viarme, Intendant of Brittany, March 22, 1740. A.D. d'Ille-et-Vilaine, C. 1835.

11. Sénéchaussée of Ploermel to Camus de Pontcarré de Viarme, Intendant of Brittany, June 13, 1740. A.D. d'Ille-et-Vilaine, C. 1836.

12. Sénéchaussées of Béarn to Maupeou, 1772. A.D. des Pyrénées-Atlantiques, C. 1323.

13. "Moyens de remettre en crédit les charges du Présidial de Nantes," April 3, 1740. A.D. d'Ille-et-Vilaine, C. 1836.

14. Sénéchaussée of Guérande to Camus de Pontcarré de Viarme, August 1740. A.D. d'Ille-et-Vilaine, C. 1835.

15. "Mémoire pour les officiers de la sénéchaussée et siège présidial de Nantes," April 3, 1740. A.D. d'Ille-et-Vilaine, C. 1836.

16. Ibid.

17. Maupeou (the elder) to Guignard de Saint-Priest, Intendant of Langue-doc, February 22, 1766. A.D. de l'Hérault, C. 60.

18. "Etat des dettes dont sont chargés les officiers du Présidial de Limoux, avec une notte de chaque acte d'emprunte avec l'emploi," October 1766. A.D. de l'Hérault, C. 60.

19. "Mémoire pour les officiers . . . de Nantes," April 1740. A.D. d'Ille-et-Vilaine, C. 1836.

20. Sénéchaussées of Béarn to Maupeou, 1772. A.D. des Pyrénées-Atlantiques, C. 1323.

21. "Mémoire pour les officiers . . . de Nantes," April 1740. A.D. d'Ille-et-Vilaine, C. 1836.

22. "Avis de l'intendant [Nicolas de Lamoignon de Basville] sur les contesta-tions entre les officiers du Présidial de Nîmes et la Princesse de L'Islebonne, du-chesse de Joyeuse, au sujet de l'indemnité réclamée par ces officiers à cause de la distraction de leur ressort de la terre de Joyeuse érigée en duché," May 21, 1715. A.D. de l'Hérault, C. 69A.

23. D'Aguesseau to Intendant of Franche-Comté, June 3, 1740. A.D. de la Haute-Saône, C. 82.

24. Minutes of the Estates of Languedoc, December 1743–February 1744. A.D. de la Haute-Garonne, C. 2388.

25. "Mémoire sur l'état actuel du Siège présidial et la sénéchaussée de Béziers et des justices royalles et banneretes de son ressort," February 15, 1753. A.D. de l'Hérault, C. 69B.

26. "Mémoire pour la conservation du Sénéchal et Présidial de Limoux," 1769. A.D. de l'Hérault, C. 52.

27. "Mémoire pour les officiers . . . de Nantes," April 1740. A.D. d'Ille-et-Vilaine, C. 1836.

28. Maguelone de St. Benoit, "Mémoire," to Guignard de Saint-Priest, In-tendant of Languedoc, October 10, 1766. A.D. de l'Hérault, C. 60.

29. Laval de La Crène to Rossignol, Intendant of Auvergne. A.D. du Puy-de-Dôme, C. 7682. Reference from *Inventaire-sommaire des Archives Départementales, Puy-de-Dôme. Antérieures à 1790,* Série C (Clermont-Ferrand, 1893–1916), V, 377; original not consulted.

30. Text of enactment reproduced in appendix to Arthur Michel de Boislisle, ed., *Correspondance des contrôleurs généraux des finances avec les intendants des provinces* (Paris, 1874–1897), I, 565–574.

31. Pierre Goubert, "Les officiers royaux des présidiaux, bailliages et élections dans la société française du XVII<sup>e</sup> siècle," *Dix-septième siècle. Bulletin de la Société d'études du XVII<sup>e</sup> siècle,* 42 (1959), 66.

32. "Mémoire présenté au roi par le Présidial de Nîmes réclamant la no-blesse," 1782. A.D. de la Drôme, B. 629.

33. "Raisons générales et particulières du dépérissement des charges de judi-cature, de leur décry [sic], et, par conséquent, du dégoût général pour les posséder," April 25, 1740. A.D. d'Ille-et-Vilaine, C. 1835.

34. "Moyens de remettre en crédit les charges . . . de Nantes," April 1740. A.D. d'Ille-et-Vilaine, C. 1836.

35. Maguelone de St. Benoit, "Mémoire," October 1766. A.D. de l'Hérault, C. 60.

36. Maguelone de St. Benoit, "Etat du Présidial et Sénéchaussée de Limoux ressortissant au Parlement de Toulouse dans le cas où il juge à la charge de

l'appel. Créé par édit de 1642," December 2, 1760; Maguelone de St. Benoit, "Plan de répartition des gages à attribuer aux offices du Présidial et Sénéchaussée de Limoux en Languedoc à conserver suivant les différents projets proposés dans les observations et mémoire ci joints," October 10, 1766. A.D. de l'Hérault, C. 60.

37. Maguelone de St. Benoit, "Mémoire," October 1766. A.D. de l'Hérault, C. 60.

38. Maguelone de St. Benoit, "Supplément au plan et mémoire concernant le projet de faire rendre gratuitement la justice en France, envoyé à M. l'Intendant le 10 octobre 1766. Servant de réponse aux observations contenues dans sa lettre du 22, du même mois," October 31, 1766. A.D. de l'Hérault, C. 60.

39. "Mémoire sur l'etat actuel du Siège . . . de Béziers," February 1753. A.D. de l'Hérault, C. 69B.

40. "Réflexions essentielles pour former ou rectifier un plan de rétablissement des sièges présidiaux et sénéchaussées," June 21, 1753. A.D. de l'Hérault, C. 69B.

41. "Copie des représentations faites à M. le Chancelier de France, par les officiers du Sénéchal et Présidial de Caors," May 1754. A.D. du Lot, C. 215.

42. Sénéchaussée of Lannion, "Moyens qui paroissent les moins onéreux au public pour remettre les charges en vigueur," June 19, 1740. A.D. d'Ille-et-Vilaine, C. 1835.

43. Guignard de Saint-Priest, "Mémoire sur le rétablissement du Présidial et du Sénéchal de Montpellier, ensemble de toutes les autres sièges royaux de la province," 1755. A.D. de l'Hérault, C. 69B.

44. Nicolas-Simon-Henri Linguet, *Nécessité d'une réforme dans l'administration de la justice et dans les loix civiles en France, avec la réfutation de quelques passages de L'esprit des loix* (Amsterdam, 1764), p. 52.

45. Ibid., pp. 51, 62.

46. Ibid., pp. 71–72, 77.

47. Laurain, *Essai sur les présidiaux,* pp. 70–71; Philip Dawson, *Provincial Magistrates and Revolutionary Politics in France, 1789–1795* (Cambridge, Mass.: Harvard University Press, 1972), pp. 57–58.

48. "Mémoire sur l'état actuel du Siège . . . de Béziers," February 1753. A.D. de l'Hérault, C. 69B.

49. See Laurain, *Essai sur les présidiaux,* pp. 86–94; and Dawson, *Provincial Magistrates,* pp. 63–64. See also William Doyle, *The Parlement of Bordeaux and the End of the Old Regime, 1771–1790* (New York: St. Martin's Press, 1974), pp. 217–219.

50. The chancellors of France in the eighteenth century were: Pontchartrain (1699–1714); Voysin (1714–1717); d'Aguesseau (1717–1750, in exile 1718–1720 and 1722–1727); Lamoignon de Blancmesnil (1750–1768, in exile 1763–1768); and Maupeou the younger (1768–1790, in exile 1774–1790). The keepers of the seals were: Pontchartrain (1699–1714); Voysin (1714–1717); d'Aguesseau (1717–1718); Marc-René de Voyer d'Argenson (1718–1720); d'Aguesseau (1720–1722); Armenonville (1722–1727); Chauvelin (1727–1737); d'Aguesseau (1737–1750); Machault (1750–1757); Louis XV (1757–1760); Berryer (1761–1762); Feydeau de Brou (1762–1763); Maupeou the elder (1763–1768); Maupeou the younger (1768–1774); Miromesnil (1774–1787); Lamoignon de Basville (1787–1788); Barentin (1788–1789); Champion de Cicé (1789–1790); and Duport-Dutertre (1790).

51. See J. M. J. Rogister, "Conflict and Harmony in Eighteenth-Century

France: A Reappraisal of the Nature of the Relations between the Crown and the Parlement of Paris (1730–1754)" (Ph.D. thesis, Oxford University, 1971).

52. Dawson, *Provincial Magistrates,* pp. 55–56.

53. See Jean-André Tournerie, *Recherches sur la crise judiciaire en province à la fin de l'Ancien régime: Le Présidial de Tours de 1740 à 1790* (Tours: Faculté des Sciences juridiques et économiques, 1975).

54. "Mémoire sur le rétablissement du Présidial de Montpellier," October 1752. A.D. de l'Hérault, C. 69B.

55. Guignard de Saint-Priest, "Mémoire sur le rétablissement du Présidial . . . de Montpellier," 1755. A.D. de l'Hérault, C. 69B.

56. Guillaume-François Le Trosne, *Discours sur l'état actuel de la magistrature, et sur les causes de sa décadence. Prononcé à l'ouverture des audiences du Bailliage d'Orléans, le 15 novembre 1763* (Paris, 1764), pp. 86–87.

*4. A Misfeatured Attempt at Reform and Its Aftermath*

1. Voltaire, "L'équivoque" (1771), *Oeuvres complètes,* ed. Morland (1877–1885), XXVIII, 423.

2. See Jules Flammermont, *La réforme judiciaire du Chancelier Maupeou, mémoire lu à l'Académie des sciences morales et politiques, en novembre et décembre 1879* (Paris, 1880), pp. 21–22; Flammermont, *Le Chancelier Maupeou et les parlements,* pp. 214–215; and William O. Doyle, "The Parlements of France and the Breakdown of the Old Regime," *French Historical Studies,* 6 (1970), 415–418. It is to be noted, however, that Flammermont inclined toward the view that Maupeou knew what he was about (*Le Chancelier Maupeou et les parlements,* p. 285). Other works depicting Maupeou as a purposeful reformer, but also expressing approval of him, which Flammermont did not: François Piétri, *La réforme de l'état au XVIIIe siècle* (Paris: Les Editions de France, 1935), p. 36; Alfred Cobban, "The Parlements of France in the Eighteenth Century," *History,* 35 (1950), 64–80; and David Carl Hudson, *Maupeou and the Parlements: A Study in Propaganda and Politics* (Ann Arbor: University Microfilms, 1968).

3. See Charles-François Lebrun, *Opinions, et choix d'écrits politiques, de Charles-François Lebrun, duc de Plaisance, recueillis et mis en ordre par son fils ainé et précédés d'une notice biographique,* ed. Anne-Charles Lebrun (Paris, 1829), especially pp. 179–181.

4. Martin Mansergh, "The Revolution of 1771; or, The Exile of the Parlement of Paris" (Ph.D. thesis, Oxford University, 1973), pp. 133–136.

5. Nicolas-Simon-Henri Linguet, *Réflexions sur la résistance opposée à l'exécution des ordonnances promulguées le 8 mai 1788; Suivies de la différence entre la révolution passagère de 1771, et la réforme de 1788, dans l'ordre judiciaire en France* (Brussels, 1788), pp. 94–95.

6. "Letters of Joseph II," *The Pamphleteer; Dedicated to Both Houses of Parliament* (London), 19 (1822), 86–87. German original in Joseph II, *Briefe,* 3rd ed., ed. Franz Schuselka (Leipzig, 1846), pp. 34–35.

7. Maupeou, "Mémoire de Maupeou à Louis XVI" (1789), in Flammermont, *Le Chancelier Maupeou et les parlements,* pp. 599–646.

8. See Lebrun, *Opinions, et choix d'écrits politiques,* ed. Lebrun (1829), pp. 171–199.

9. Maupeou, "Mémoire de Maupeou à Louis XVI" (1789), in Flammermont, *Le Chancelier Maupeou et les parlements,* p. 632.

10. Saint-Pierre, *Ouvrajes de politique* (1733–1741), VII, 78–79. In the sixteenth century, the Estates-General had called for more parlements in the ressort of the

Parlement of Paris, though not according to any geometrical plan. Raoul Spifame's 1556 work, *Dicaearchiae Henrici regis christianissimi progymnasmata,* echoed those calls. A selection from Spifame's work was reprinted in 1775, but the editor did not include Spifame's ideas for redividing the jurisdiction of the Parlement. See Jeanclos, *Les projets de réforme judiciaire de Raoul Spifame,* pp. 66–74, 110–111.

11. The symmetry of Maupeou's plan was somewhat marred in late 1771, when, after many protests, he agreed to create a conseil supérieur at Douai to replace the old Parlement of Flanders, which he had suppressed. The chancellor had intended originally to have for this northern region only one conseil supérieur, at Arras (seat of the former Conseil d'Artois, from which appeals had gone to the Parlement of Paris). See Gabriel-Maximilien-Louis Pillot, *Histoire du Parlement de Flandres* (Douai, 1849–1850), I, 16–17, 324–329.

12. Lebrun, *Opinions, et choix d'écrits politiques,* ed. Lebrun (1829), p. 180.

13. Maupeou, "Mémoire de Maupeou à Louis XVI" (1789), in Flammermont, *Le Chancelier Maupeou et les parlements,* p. 609.

14. For summaries of the Maupeou reforms, see the works cited above of Flammermont, Doyle, and Mansergh, and see also Jean Egret, *Louis XV et l'opposition parlementaire* (Paris: Armand Colin, 1970), pp. 182–202.

15. Maupeou, "Mémoire de Maupeou à Louis XVI" (1789), in Flammermont, *Le Chancelier Maupeou et les parlements,* pp. 613, 617.

16. Guy-Jean-Baptiste Target, *Lettres d'un homme à un autre homme sur l'extinction de l'ancien Parlement, et la création du nouveau* (n.p., 1771), p. 6. See also Diderot, *Mémoires pour Cathérine II* (1773), ed. Vernière (1966), pp. 3–35; l'abbé Claude Mey, *Maximes du droit public français, tirées des capitulaires, des ordonnances du royaume,* 2nd ed. (Amsterdam, 1775), especially pp. 1–5, 130, 254; and Louis Léon Félicité, duc de Brancas, *Extrait du droit publique de la France* (n.p., 1771), especially pp. 14–16, 57–58, 72.

17. Guy-Jean-Baptiste Target, *Lettres d'un homme à un autre homme sur les affaires du temps* (n.p., 1771), p. 27.

18. Maupeou, "Mémoire de Maupeou à Louis XVI" (1789), in Flammermont, *Le Chancelier Maupeou et les parlements,* pp. 632–644.

19. See Henri Carré, "Turgot et le rappel des parlements," *La Révolution française,* XXII (1902), 193–208.

20. Beaumarchais to M. de Sartines, November 14, 1774, in Pierre Augustin Caron de Beaumarchais, *Correspondance,* ed. Brian N. Morton (Paris: A. G. Nizet, 1969), II, 118.

21. See Bailey Stillman Stone, *Crisis in the Paris Parlement: the Grand'Chambriers, 1774–1789* (Ann Arbor: University Microfilms, 1973), pp. 42–44.

22. Diderot, *Mémoires pour Cathérine II* (1773), ed. Vernière (1966), pp. 32–33.

23. Flammermont, *Le Chancelier Maupeou et les parlements,* p. 405.

24. Armand-Thomas Hue de Miromesnil, "Etat de la Magistrature" (1772), Ms. fr. 10986, Bibliothèque Nationale.

25. Joseph Michaud, *Biographie universelle, ancienne et moderne,* new ed. (Paris, 1842–1865), XXVIII, pp. 395–396.

26. Miromesnil, "Etat de la Magistrature" (1772), fols. 4, 27, 58, 69.

27. See Laurain, *Essai sur les présidiaux,* pp. 91–94.

28. *Très-humbles et très-respectueuses représentations des officiers du bailliage et siège présidiale [sic] de Vitry-le-Fançois [sic] à Monseigneur le Garde des sceaux sur l'Edit du Roi portant réglement pour la jurisdiction des présidiaux du mois d'Aôut [sic] 1777* (Vitry-le-François, n. d.). A.D. de la Marne, C. 1771. Subsequent references are to pp. 3, 14, 23–24, 50–51.

29. Isambert et al., eds., *Recueil général des anciennes lois françaises*, XXV, p. 85.

30. Présidial of Auxerre to Charles-Henri Feydeau de Brou, Intendant of Burgundy, July 1783. A.D. de l'Yonne, C. 3.

31. "Mémoire présenté à Monseigneur l'Intendant de Bourgogne par les officiers du Bailliage et siège Présidial d'Auxerre"; "Mémoire pour les officiers du Bailliage et siège Présidial d'Auxerre," July 1783. A.D. de l'Yonne, C. 3.

32. "Observations des Officiers au Bailliage et siège Présidial d'Auxerre sur le projet arrêté aux derniers Etats de la province de Bourgogne d'enlever à leur siège la connoissance par appel des jugemens de police"; "Mémoire pour les officiers . . . d'Auxerre," July 1783. A.D. de l'Yonne, C. 3.

33. "Mémoire pour les officiers titulaires au Bailliage et siège Présidiale d'Auxerre," July 1783. A.D. de l'Yonne, C. 3.

34. "Mémoire présenté à Monseigneur l'Intendant de Bourgogne par les officiers du Bailliage et siège Présidial d'Auxerre," July 1783. A.D. de l'Yonne, C. 3.

*5. Views toward the Reconstruction of the Judiciary on the Eve of Revolution*

1. Nicolas-Simon-Henri Linguet, *Aiguilloniana; ou Anecdotes utiles pour l'histoire de France, au dix-huitième siècle, depuis l'année 1770* (London, 1777), p. 44.

2. Ibid., pp. 122–123.

3. Ibid., pp. 46–49.

4. Antoine Léonard Thomas, *Oeuvres complètes de Thomas, de l'Académie française*, ed. Saint-Surin (Paris, 1825), III, 203, 208.

5. Ibid., pp. 203–204.

6. Ibid., p. 243.

7. Ibid., pp. 320–321, 382–383.

8. François-Joseph-Mamert de Jussieu de Montluel, *Réflexions sur les principes de la justice* (Paris, 1761), p. 118.

9. Michaud, *Biographie universelle*, XXI, p. 359.

10. Louis-Bernard Guyton de Morveau, *Lettre à M*** où l'on développe le plan annoncé dans le Discours sur l'état actuel de la jurisprudence, pour parvenir à la rendre simple, uniforme, universelle, et constante. A Dijon ce 19 mars 1771*, in *Discours publics et éloges, aux quels on a joint une lettre où l'auteur développe le plan annoncé dans l'un de ses discours pour réformer la jurisprudence* (Paris, 1775–1782), I, 156.

11. Ibid., p. 138.

12. Merle L. Perkins, "Voltaire and the Abbé de Saint-Pierre," *The French Review*, 34 (1960), 162.

13. Alan Charles Kors, *D'Holbach's Coterie: An Enlightenment in Paris* (Princeton: Princeton University Press, 1976), p. 319.

14. Frederick Copleston, *A History of Philosophy* (London: Search Press, 1946–1975), VI, part 1, pp. 51–52.

15. Voltaire, *Oeuvres complètes*, ed. Morland (1877–1885), XIV, 514.

16. Balteau et al., *Dictionnaire de biographie*, VIII, 745–746.

17. Jean-François Marmontel, *Bélisaire* (Paris, 1767), p. 100. Subsequent translations are from Jean-François Marmontel, *Belisarius: A Tale*, trans. anon. (London, 1818), pp. 82–83, 94, 110, 118–119. References in Fr. orig. pp. 97, 111, 130, 140–141.

18. Joseph-Michel-Antoine Servan, *Des révolutions dans les grandes sociétés civiles, considérées dans leurs rapports avec l'ordre* (written ca. 1795), in *Oeuvres choisies de Servan. Nouvelle édition augmentée de plusieurs pièces inédites*, ed. Xavier de Portets (Paris, 1822), V, 87.

19. Joseph-Michel-Antoine Servan, *Discours sur l'administration de la justice criminelle* (Geneva, 1767), p. 118.

20. Ibid., pp. 122–123.

21. Servan, *Discours sur le progrès des connoissances humaines* (1781), pp. 72–75.

22. Joseph-Michel-Antoine Servan, *Réflexions sur quelques points de nos loix, à l'occasion d'un événement important* (Geneva, 1781), pp. 199, 201.

23. Servan, *Commentaires historiques et critiques sur les deux premiers livres des Essais de Montaigne* (written ca. 1800), in *Oeuvres choisies de Servan*, ed. de Portets (1822), IV, 452.

24. Ibid., p. 466.

25. The surviving unpublished essays and other materials pertaining to the competition, including summaries and critiques of some of the essays by members of the academy, are in A.D. de la Marne, 1 J 49. All references below, unless otherwise noted, are to materials under this *cote*.

26. Michaud, *Biographie universelle*, XVII, 282–283.

27. Balteau et al., *Dictionnaire de biographie*, VII, 607.

28. Jérôme Pétion de Villeneuve, *Les lois civiles et l'administration de la justice ramenées à un ordre simple et uniforme; ou Réflexions morales, politiques, etc., etc., sur la manière de rendre la justice en France avec le plus de célérité et le moins de frais possibles* (London, 1782). Reprinted in Jérôme Pétion de Villeneuve, *Oeuvres* (Paris, 1792–1793), I. References below will be to one edition or the other, as designated.

29. Bucquet, *Discours qui a remporté le prix à l'Académie de Chaalons* (1789).

30. Ibid., p. 7.

31. Ibid., p. 4.

32. Pétion de Villeneuve, *Les lois civiles et l'administration de la justice* (1782), p. 12.

33. See also Daniel Jousse, *Traité de l'administration de la justice* (Paris, 1771), I, xx–xxi.

34. Pétion de Villeneuve, *Les lois civiles et l'administration de la justice*, in *Oeuvres* (1792–1793), I, 185–206.

35. Ibid., p. 203.

36. For Lamoignon and the reform of 1788, see Marcel Marion, *Le garde des sceaux Lamoignon et la réforme judiciaire de 1788* (Paris: Hachette, 1905); Henri Carré, *La fin des parlements (1788–1790)* (Paris: Hachette, 1912); and Jean Egret, *La Pré-Révolution française (1787–1788)* (Paris: Presses universitaires de France, 1962).

37. Joseph-Dominique-Elzéar de Bernardi de Valernes, *Essai sur les révolutions du droit français pour servir d'introduction à l'étude de ce droit; suivi de vues sur la justice civile, au projet de réformation dans l'administration de la justice civile* (Paris, 1785), pp. 362–366.

38. Balteau et al., *Dictionnaire de biographie*, V, 231–232.

39. Claude-Gaspard Barbat du Closel d'Arnery, *Projet d'édit pour la restauration de la chose publique, la convocation régulière des états généraux, la restauration des anciennes cours plenières, le rappel des parlements . . . la suppression de la vénalité des charges, des committimus et de tous les tribunaux d'exception. Ouvrage précédé des lettres adressées à Leurs Majestés, et suivi de l'esquisse d'un code uniforme pour tout le royaume, par l'auteur de L'Abus et des dangers de la contrainte par corps* (n.p., 1788), pp. 5–62.

40. Bernardi, *Essai sur les révolutions du droit français* (1785), pp. 366–370.

41. Charles-Louis de Secondat, baron de la Brède et de Montesquieu, *De l'esprit des lois* (1748), ed. Gonzague Truc (Paris: Garnier, 1961), I, 19–22; II, 21–22 (Book II, chap. 4; Book XX, chap. 22).

42. Diderot, *Mémoires pour Cathérine II* (1773), ed. Vernière (1966), pp. 17, 24.

43. Linguet, *Réflexions sur la résistance opposée à l'exécution des ordonnances promulguées le 8 mai 1788* (1788), p. 94.
44. John Arthur Mourant, *The Physiocratic Conception of Natural Law* (Chicago: University of Chicago, 1943), p. 53.
45. Denis Richet, *La France moderne: L'esprit des institutions* (Paris: Flammarion, 1973), pp. 157–159; Mario Einaudi, *The Physiocratic Doctrine of Judicial Control* (Cambridge, Mass.: Harvard University Press, 1938), pp. 50–53, 69–72.
46. Otto Gierke, *Natural Law and the Theory of Society*, trans. Ernest Barker (Cambridge, Eng.: Cambridge University Press, 1934; German orig. 1913), I, 162–195.

*Conclusion*

1. See Raoul Aubin, *L'organisation judiciaire d'après les cahiers de 1789* (Paris: Jouve, 1928).
2. Jérôme Mavidal et al., eds., *Archives parlementaires de 1787 à 1860, recueil complet des débats législatifs et politiques des chambres françaises*, 1st series, 1787–1799 (Paris, 1867–1913), VIII, 440–450.
3. Ibid., p. 449.
4. Edmond Seligman, *La justice en France pendant la Révolution* (Paris: Plon-Nourrit, 1901–1913), I, 197. Other works on the Revolutionary period are Jean Bourdon, *La réforme judiciaire de l'an VIII* (Rodez: Carrère, 1941), 2 vols.; and André-Jean Arnaud, *Les origines doctrinales du Code civil français* (Paris: Librairie Générale de Droit et de Jurisprudence, 1969).
5. Mavidal et al., eds., *Archives parlementaires*, 1st series, 1787–1799, XII, 348–349.
6. *Les véritables intérêts de la nation, considérés dans la vente des biens ecclésiastiques, et dans la destruction de la noblesse et des parlements. Par un citoyen impartial.* (Paris, 1790), p. 76.
7. See Mavidal et al., eds., *Archives parlementaires*, 1st series, 1787–1799, X, XI, XII, XV, XVI, XVII.
8. Jeremy Bentham, *Draught of a New Plan for the Organisation of the Judicial Establishment in France; Proposed as a Succedaneum to the Draught Presented for the Same Purpose by the Committee of Constitution to the National Assembly, December 21ˢᵗ, 1789* (n.p., 1790).
9. Mavidal et al., eds., *Archives parlementaires*, 1st series, 1787–1799, XV, 361.
10. Ibid., p. 680.
11. Ibid., XII, 345.
12. Ibid., p. 421.
13. Linguet, *Nécessité d'une réforme dans l'administration de la justice* (1764), pp. 70–71.
14. Camille Pagé, *La coutellerie depuis l'origine jusqu'à nos jours* (Châtellerault, 1896–1904), IV, 640, 663, 664, 668, 672, 676.

# Works Cited

*Manuscripts*

*Archives départementales*
### Côte-d'Or
C. 4. Letter from d'Aguesseau to La Briffe, Intendant of Burgundy, January 25, 1740.
### Drôme
B. 629. Memorial from the Présidial of Nîmes demanding nobility, 1782.
### Haute-Garonne
C. 2388. Minutes of the Estates of Languedoc, December 1743–February 1744.
### Haute-Saône
C. 82. Letter from d'Aguesseau to the Intendant of Franche-Comté, June 3, 1740.
### Hérault
C. 52. Memorial from the Présidial of Limoux, 1769.
C. 60. Memoirs from Maguelone de St. Benoit, judge in the Présidial of Limoux, 1760, 1766; Letter from Maupeou the elder to Guignard de Saint-Priest, Intendant of Languedoc, February 22, 1766.
C. 69A. Memoir from Nicolas de Lamoignon de Basville, Intendant of Languedoc, on a dispute between the Présidial of Nîmes and the Princesse de L'Islebonne, May 21, 1715.
C. 69B. Memoirs on the Présidiaux of Montpellier, Béziers, and others, 1752–1755.
### Ille-et-Vilaine
C. 1835. Memorials from the Présidiaux of Vannes and Quimper, the Sénéchaussées of Lannion and Guérande, and the Bailliage of Châteaulin to Camus de Pontcarré de Viarme, Intendant of Brittany, 1740.
C. 1836. Letters and memorials from the Présidial of Nantes and the Sénéchaussée of Ploermel to Camus de Pontcarré de Viarme, 1740.
### Lot
C. 215. Memorial from the Présidial of Caors to Lamoignon de Blancmesnil, May 1754.
### Marne
C. 1771. Memorial from the Présidial of Vitry-le-François to Miromesnil, August 1777.
1 J 49. Essays submitted to the Academy of Châlons-sur-Marne for a competition in 1782 on the question: "What would be the means of rendering justice in France with the most celerity and the least cost possible?"
### Pyrénées-Atlantiques
C. 1323. Memorial from the sénéchaussées of Béarn to Maupeou, 1772.
### Yonne
C. 3. Memorials from the Présidial of Auxerre to the Intendant of Burgundy, 1783.

*Bibliothèque Nationale*
Ms. fr. 10986. Armand-Thomas Hue de Miromesnil, "Etat de la Magistrature," 1772.

*Bibliothèque Sainte-Geneviève*
Ms. 825. Michel de Marillac, "Mémoire dressé principalement contre l'autorité du Parlement," undated.

*Published Works*

*Primary Sources*
Aguesseau, Henri-François d'. *Lettres inédites du chancelier d'Aguesseau.* Edited by D. B. Rives. 2 vol. Paris, 1823.
——— *Mémoire inédit du chancelier Daguesseau sur la réformation de la justice.* Edited by Paule Combe. Valence: Imprimés réunies, 1928.
——— *Oeuvres complètes du chancelier d'Aguesseau.* Edited by Jean-Marie Pardessus. 16 vols. Paris, 1819.
Argenson, René-Louis de Voyer, marquis d'. *Considérations sur le gouvernement ancien et présent de la France.* Amsterdam, 1765.
——— *Journal et mémoires du marquis d'Argenson.* Edited by Edme Jacques Benoît Rathéry. 9 vols. Paris, 1859–1867.
——— *Mémoires et journal inédit du marquis d'Argenson, ministre des affaires étrangères sous Louis XV.* Edited by Charles Marc René de Voyer, marquis d'Argenson. 5 vols. Paris, 1857–1858.
Aristotle. *Problems II: Rhetorica ad Alexandrum.* Translated by W. S. Hett and H. Rackham. Loeb Classical Library. Cambridge, Mass.: Harvard University Press, 1965.
Barbat du Closel d'Arnery, Claude-Gaspard. *Projet d'édit pour la restauration de la chose publique, la convocation régulière des états généraux, la restauration des anciennes cours plenières, le rappel des parlements . . . la suppression de la vénalité des charges, des committimus et de tous les tribunaux d'exception. Ouvrage précédé des lettres adressées à Leurs Majestés, et suivi de l'esquisse d'un code uniforme pour tout le royaume, par l'auteur de L'abus et des dangers de la contrainte par corps.* N. p., 1788.
Beaumarchais, Pierre Augustin Caron de. *Correspondance.* Edited by Brian N. Morton. 3 vols. Paris: A. G. Nizet, 1969.
Bentham, Jeremy. *Draught of a New Plan for the Organisation of the Judicial Establishment in France; Proposed as a Succedaneum to the Draught Presented for the Same Purpose by the Committee of Constitution to the National Assembly, December 21$^{st}$, 1789.* N. p., 1790.
Bernardi de Valernes, Joseph-Dominique-Elzéar de. *Essai sur les révolutions du droit français pour servir d'introduction à l'étude de ce droit; suivi de vues sur la justice civile, au projet de réformation dans l'administration de la justice civile.* Paris, 1785.
Besenval, Pierre Victor, baron de. *Mémoires de M. le baron de Besenval.* Edited by Alexandre-Joseph Pierre, vicomte de Ségur. 4 vols. Paris, 1805–1807.
Bodin, Jean. *The Six Bookes of a Commonweale.* Translated by Richard Knolles (1606). Edited by Kenneth Douglas McRae. Cambridge, Mass.: Harvard University Press, 1962.
Boislisle, Arthur Michel de, ed. *Correspondance des contrôleurs généraux des finances avec les intendants des provinces.* 3 vols. Paris, 1874–1897.
Bonet, Philibert. *Moyens pour abreger les procès et oster les empeschemens de bonne et brefve expedition de iustice.* Paris, 1556.
Brancas, Louis Léon Félicité, duc de. *Extrait du droit publique de la France.* N.p., 1771.
Bretonnier, Barthélemy-Joseph. *Recueil par ordre alphabétique des principales questions de droit, qui se jugent diversement dans les différens tribunaux du royaume. Avec des réflexions pour concilier la diversité de la jurisprudence, et la rendre uniforme dans tous les tribunaux.* 3rd ed. 2 vols. Paris, 1752–1753.

Bucquet, Louis-Jean-Baptiste. *Discours qui a remporté le prix à l'Académie de Chaalons, en l'année M.DCC.LXXXIII. Sur cette question proposée par la même académie: Quels seroient les moyens de rendre la justice en France avec le plus de célérité et le moins de frais possibles?* Beauvais, 1789.

Cappel, Ange. *L'advis donne au roy sur l'abréviation des procès.* Paris? ca. 1600.

Commynes, Philippe de. *Mémoires.* Edited by Joseph Calmette. 3 vols. Paris: H. Champion, 1924–1925.

Coquille, Guy. *Les oeuvres de Maistre Guy de Coquille, Sieur de Romenay, contenant plusieurs traitez touchant les libertez de l'Eglise gallicane, l'histoire de France et le droit françois.* Edited by Claude Labottiere. 2 vols. Bordeaux, 1703.

Coras, Jean de. *Discours des parties et office d'un bon et entier juge.* Lyon, 1618.

Descartes, René. *Oeuvres philosophiques.* Edited by Ferdinand Alquié. 3 vols. Paris: Garnier, 1963–1973.

Diderot, Denis. *Mémoires pour Cathérine II.* Edited by Paul Vernière. Paris: Garnier, 1966.

Domat, Jean. *Les loix civiles dans leur ordre naturel.* 2nd ed. 3 vols. Paris, 1696–1697.

———— *Oeuvres complètes de Jean Domat.* Edited by Joseph Rémy. 4 vols. Paris, 1828–1830.

Du Noyer, François. *Articles, que presente au roy François du Noyer Escuyer sieur de S. Martin, pour establir une compagnie, afin de rendre la iustice gratuitement en France, et regler les benefices, oster la venalité des offices et charges. Avec les moyens pour y parvenir approuvez par les Estats Generaux n'agueres tenus en la ville de Paris.* Paris, 1616.

Figon, Charles de. *Discours des estats et offices, tant du gouvernement que de la justice et des finances de France.* Paris, 1608.

Fontenelle, Bernard le Bovier de. *Oeuvres de Fontenelle.* Edited by G. B. Depping. 3 vols. Paris, 1818.

Guyton de Morveau, Louis-Bernard. *Discours publics et éloges, aux quels on a joint une lettre où l'auteur développe le plan annoncé dans l'un de ses discours pour réformer la jurisprudence.* 3 vols. Paris, 1775–1782.

Hotman, François. *Francogallia.* Edited and translated by Ralph E. Giesey and J. H. M. Salmon. Cambridge, Eng.: Cambridge University Press, 1972.

*Inventaire-sommaire des Archives Départementales, Puy-de-Dôme. Antérieures à 1790,* Series C. 6 vols. Clermont-Ferrand, 1893–1916.

Isambert, François André, et al., eds. *Recueil général des anciennes lois françaises, depuis l'an 420 jusqu'à la Révolution de 1789.* 29 vols. Paris, 1821–1833.

Jousse, Daniel. *Traité de l'administration de la justice.* 2 vols. Paris, 1771.

Jussieu de Montluel, François-Joseph-Mamert de. *Réflexions sur les principes de la justice.* Paris, 1761.

Labitte, Jacques. *Règlement pour la réformation et abbréviation de la iustice du Duché de Mayne et sieges qui en dépendent.* Paris, 1582.

La Bruyère, Jean de. *Characters.* Translated by Jean Stewart. Baltimore: Penguin Books, 1970.

La Popelinière, Lancelot Voysin, sieur de. *L'histoire de France enrichie des plus notables occurrances survenues ez provinces de l'Europe et pays voisins, soit en paix soit en guerre: tant pour le fait seculier qu'eclesiastic: depuis lan 1550 jusques a ces temps.* 2 vols. La Rochelle, 1581.

Law, John. *Oeuvres complètes.* Edited by Paul Harsin. 3 vols. Paris: Librairie du Recueil Sirey, 1934.

Lebrun, Charles-François. *Opinions, et choix d'écrits politiques, de Charles-François Lebrun, duc de Plaisance, recueillis et mis en ordre par son fils ainé et précédés d'une notice biographique.* Edited by Anne-Charles Lebrun. Paris, 1829.

*Le labyrinthe de l'estat, ou les veritables causes des malheurs de la France. A Ctesiphon.*
   Paris, 1652.
Le Trosne, Guillaume-François. *Discours sur l'état actuel de la magistrature, et sur les
   causes de sa décadence. Prononcé à l'ouverture des audiences du Bailliage d'Orléans, le
   15 novembre 1763.* Paris, 1764.
"Letters of Joseph II," *The Pamphleteer; Dedicated to Both Houses of Parliament* (Lon-
   don), 19 (1822): 79–96, 274–296.
L'Hospital, Michel. *Oeuvres complètes de Michel L'Hospital, chancelier de France.*
   Edited by P. J. S. Duféy. 3 vols. Paris, 1824–1825.
———— *Oeuvres inédites de Michel L'Hospital, chancelier de France.* Edited by P. J. S.
   Duféy. 2 vols. Paris, 1825–1826.
Linguet, Nicolas-Simon-Henri. *Aiguilloniana; ou Anecdotes utiles pour l'histoire de
   France, au dix-huitième siècle, depuis l'année 1770.* London, 1777.
———— *Nécessité d'une réforme dans l'administration de la justice et dans les loix civiles en
   France, avec la réfutation de quelques passages de L'esprit des loix.* Amsterdam,
   1764.
———— *Réflexions sur la résistance opposée à l'exécution des ordonnances promulguées le 8
   mai 1788; Suivies de la différence entre la révolution passagère de 1771, et la réforme de
   1788, dans l'ordre judiciaire en France.* Brussels, 1788.
[Loisel, Antoine]. *De l'oeil des rois et de la iustice. Remonstrance faite en la ville de Bor-
   deaux à l'ouverture de la cour de iustice envoyée par le roy en ses païs et Duché de
   Guienne.* Paris, 1584.
Loyseau, Charles. *Les oeuvres de Maistre Charles Loyseau, avocat en parlement: Contenant
   les Cinq Livres du Droit des Offices, les Traitez des Seigneuries, des Ordres et simples
   Dignitez, du Déguerpissement et Délaissement par Hypothèque de la Garantie des
   Rentes, et des Abus des Justices de Villages.* Paris, 1678.
———— *Traité des Seigneuries.* Paris, 1608.
Machiavelli, Niccolò. *The Prince and The Discourses.* Translated by Luigi Ricci and
   Christian E. Detmold. New York: Random House, 1950.
———— *Toutes les lettres officielles et familières, celles de ses seigneurs, de ses amis et des
   siens.* Edited by Edmond Barincou. 2 vols. Paris: Gallimard, 1955.
Marmontel, Jean-François. *Bélisaire.* Paris, 1767.
———— *Belisarius: A Tale.* Translator anonymous. London, 1818.
Mavidal, Jérôme, et al., eds. *Archives parlementaires de 1787 à 1860, recueil complet des
   débats législatifs et politiques des chambres françaises.* 1st series, 1787–1799. 82
   vols. Paris, 1867–1913.
Mey, l'abbé Claude. *Maximes du droit public français, tirées des capitulaires, des ordon-
   nances du royaume.* 2nd ed. Amsterdam, 1775.
Montaigne, Michel Eyquem, seigneur de. *The Complete Essays of Montaigne,*
   Translated by Donald M. Frame. Stanford, Calif.: Stanford University
   Press, 1958.
Montesquieu, Charles-Louis de Secondat, baron de la Brède et de. *De l'esprit des
   lois.* Edited by Gonzague Truc. 2 vols. Paris: Garnier, 1961.
Pétion de Villeneuve, Jérôme. *Les lois civiles et l'administration de la justice ramenées à
   un ordre simple et uniforme; ou Réflexions morales, politiques, etc., etc., sur la manière de
   rendre la justice en France avec le plus de célérité et le moins de frais possibles.* London,
   1782.
———— *Oeuvres.* 4 vols. Paris, 1792–1793.
Rabelais, François. *The Histories of Gargantua and Pantagruel.* Translated by J. M.
   Cohen. Baltimore: Penguin Books, 1955.
Racine, Jean. *Théâtre de Racine.* Edited by Pierre Mélèse. 5 vols. Paris: Imprimerie
   nationale de France, 1951.

Richelieu, Armand Jean du Plessis, cardinal de. *Testament politique.* Edited by
    Louis André. Paris: R. Laffont, 1947.
Rousseau, Jean-Jacques. *The Political Writings of Jean-Jacques Rousseau.* Edited by
    C. E. Vaughan. 2 vols. Oxford: Blackwell, 1962.
Saint-Pierre, Charles-Irénée Castel, l'abbé de. *Mémoire pour diminuer le nombre des
    procès.* Paris, 1725.
―――― *Ouvrajes de politique.* 16 vols. Rotterdam, 1733–1741.
Savaron, Jean. *Traicté de l'annuel et venalité des offices.* Paris, 1615.
Servan, Joseph-Michel-Antoine. *Discours sur l'administration de la justice criminelle.*
    Geneva, 1767.
―――― *Discours sur le progrès des connoissances humaines en général, de la morale, et de la
    législation en particulier; lu dans une assemblée publique de l'Académie de Lyon.* N. p.,
    1781.
―――― *Oeuvres choisies de Servan. Nouvelle édition augmentée de plusieurs pièces inédites.*
    Edited by Xavier de Portets. 5 vols. Paris, 1822.
―――― *Réflexions sur quelques points de nos loix, à l'occasion d'un événement important.* Ge-
    neva, 1781.
Seyssel, Claude de. *La monarchie de France et deux autres fragments politiques.* Edited
    by Jacques Poujol. Paris: Librairie d'Argences, 1961.
Smith, Adam. *An Inquiry into the Nature and Causes of the Wealth of Nations.* Edited by
    Edward Gibbon Wakefield. 4 vols. London, 1843.
Target, Guy-Jean-Baptiste. *Lettres d'un homme à un autre homme sur les affaires du
    temps.* N.p. 1771.
―――― *Lettres d'un homme à un autre homme sur l'extinction de l'ancien parlement, et la
    création du nouveau.* N.p., 1771.
Thomas, Antoine Léonard. *Oeuvres complètes de Thomas, de l'Académie française.*
    Edited by Saint-Surin. 6 vols. Paris, 1825.
*Les véritables intérêts de la nation, considérés dans la vente des biens ecclésiastiques, et dans la
    destruction de la noblesse et des parlements. Par un citoyen impartial.* Paris, 1790.
Voltaire, François Marie Arouet de. *Oeuvres complètes de Voltaire.* Edited by Louis
    Morland. 52 vols. Paris, 1877–1885.

*Secondary Works*

Arnaud, André-Jean. *Les origines doctrinales du Code civil français.* Paris: Librairie
    Générale de Droit et de Jurisprudence, 1969.
Aubin, Raoul. *L'organisation judiciaire d'après les cahiers de 1789.* Paris: Jouve, 1928.
Balteau, J., et al., *Dictionnaire de biographie française.* Paris: Letouzey, 1933–.
Bataillard, Charles. "Tableau des principaux abus existant dans le monde judi-
    ciaire au XVIᵉ siècle," *Mémoires de la Société impériale des antiquaires de France,*
    23 (1857): 198–251.
Bloch, Marc. *French Rural History: An Essay on Its Basic Characteristics.* Translated
    by Janet Sondheimer. Berkeley, Calif.: University of California Press, 1966.
Bourdon, Jean. *La réforme judiciaire de l'an VIII.* 2 vols. Rodez: Carrère, 1941.
Braudel, Fernand. *The Mediterranean and the Mediterranean World in the Age of Philip
    II.* Translated by Siân Reynolds. 2 vols. New York: Harper & Row,
    1973.
Carré, Henri. *La fin des parlements (1788–1790).* Paris: Hachette, 1912.
―――― "Turgot et le rappel des parlements," *La Révolution française,* 22 (1902):
    193–208.
Chassaigne, Marc. "Un manuel de procédure criminelle au XVIᵉ siècle," *Revue
    des études historiques,* 79 (1913): 294–317, 402–437.
Cheyette, Frédéric. "La justice et le pouvoir royal à la fin du Moyen Age
    français," *Revue historique de droit français et étranger,* Series 4, 40 (1962):
    373–394.

Clément, Pierre. *Histoire de Colbert et de son administration.* 2 vols. Paris, 1874.

Cobban, Alfred. "The Parlements of France in the Eighteenth Century," *History,* 35 (1950): 64–80.

Collot, Claude. *L'école doctrinale de droit public de Pont-à-Mousson: Pierre Grégoire de Toulouse et Guillaume Barclay, fin du XVI^e siècle.* Paris: Librairie Générale de Droit et de Jurisprudence, 1965.

Copleston, Frederick. *A History of Philosophy.* 9 vols. London: Search Press, 1946–1975.

Dauzat, Albert, Jean Dubois, and Henri Mitterand. *Nouveau dictionnaire étymologique et historique.* Paris: Larousse, 1971.

Dawson, John Philip. "The Judges in the Bailliages and Sénéchaussées, 1763–1800: A Study of Middle-Class Office-Holders before and during the French Revolution." Ph.D. thesis, Harvard University, 1961.

———— *Provincial Magistrates and Revolutionary Politics in France, 1789–1795.* Cambridge, Mass.: Harvard University Press, 1972.

Dent, Julian. *Crisis in Finance: Crown, Finances and Society in Seventeenth-Century France.* Newton Abbot, England: David & Charles, 1973.

Dewald, Jonathon. *The Magistrates of the Parlement of Rouen, 1499–1610.* Ann Arbor: University Microfilms, 1974.

Doucet, Roger. *Les institutions de la France au XVI^e siècle.* 2 vols. Paris: Picard, 1948.

Doyle, William. *The Parlement of Bordeaux and the End of the Old Regime, 1771–1790.* New York: St. Martin's Press, 1974.

———— "The Parlements of France and the Breakdown of the Old Regime," *French Historical Studies,* 6 (1970): 415–458.

Dubois, Jean. *Lexis: Dictionnaire de la langue française.* Paris: Larousse, 1975.

Egret, Jean. *Louis XV et l'opposition parlementaire.* Paris: Armand Colin, 1970.

———— *La Pré-Révolution française (1787–1788).* Paris: Presses universitaires de France, 1962.

Einaudi, Mario. *The Physiocratic Doctrine of Judicial Control.* Cambridge, Mass.: Harvard University Press, 1938.

Evérat, Edouard. *La Sénéchaussée d'Auvergne et siège présidial de Riom au XVIII^e siècle.* Paris, 1885.

Fayard, Ennamond Dominique Nicolas. *Aperçu historique sur le Parlement de Paris.* 3 vols. Lyon and Paris, 1876–1878.

Flamholtz, Diana C. T. *Etienne Pasquier and the High Magistracy during the French Wars of Religion.* Ann Arbor: University Microfilms, 1972.

Flammermont, Jules. *Le Chancelier Maupeou et les parlements.* Paris, 1883.

———— *La réforme judiciaire du Chancelier Maupeou, mémoire lu à l'Académie des sciences morales et politiques, en novembre et décembre 1879.* (Extract from *Séances et travaux de l'Académie des sciences morales et politiques,* 114 [1880].) Paris, 1880.

Ford, Franklin L. *Robe and Sword: The Regrouping of the French Aristocracy after Louis XIV.* Cambridge, Mass.: Harvard University Press, 1953.

Frame, Donald M. *François Rabelais: A Study.* New York: Harcourt Brace Jovanovich, 1977.

Franklin, Julian H. *Jean Bodin and the Rise of Absolutist Theory.* Cambridge, Eng.: Cambridge University Press, 1973.

Fustel de Coulanges, Numa Denis. "La justice en France sous la monarchie absolue," *Revue des deux mondes,* 95 (1871): 570–601.

Garcin, Paul. "Michel de L'Hospital et les tribunaux consulaires," *Revue des deux mondes,* n.s., 16 (1963): 118–25.

Gierke, Otto. *Natural Law and the Theory of Society.* Translated by Ernest Barker. 2 vols. Cambridge, Eng.: Cambridge University Press, 1934.

Goubert, Pierre. "Les officiers royaux des présidiaux, bailliages et élections dans la société française du XVIIᵉ siècle," *Dix-septième siècle. Bulletin de la Société d'études du XVIIᵉ siècle*, 42 (1959): 54–75.

Hayden, J. Michael. *France and the Estates General of 1614.* London: Cambridge University Press, 1974.

Henry, Nannerl Overholsen. *Democratic Monarchy: The Political Thought of the Marquis d'Argenson.* Ann Arbor: University Microfilms, 1968.

Hudson, David Carl. *Maupeou and the Parlements: A Study in Propaganda and Politics.* Ann Arbor: University Microfilms, 1968.

Jeanclos, Yves. *Les projets de réforme judiciaire de Raoul Spifame au XVIᵉ siècle.* Geneva: Droz, 1977.

Keeling, S. V. *Descartes.* 2nd ed. Oxford: Oxford University Press, 1968.

Kors, Alan Charles. *D'Holbach's Coterie: An Enlightenment in Paris.* Princeton: Princeton University Press, 1976.

Kossmann, Ernest H. *La Fronde.* Leiden: Universitaire Pers Leiden, 1954.

Kunkel, Wolfgang. *An Introduction to Roman Legal and Constitutional History.* Translated by J. M. Kelly. 2nd ed. Oxford: Oxford University Press, 1973.

Laurain, Ernest. *Essai sur les présidiaux.* Paris, 1896.

Lavisse, Ernest, ed. *Histoire de France depuis les origines jusqu'à la Révolution.* 9 vols. Paris: Hachette, 1903–1911.

Littré, Emile. *Dictionnaire de la langue française.* 4 vols. Paris, 1881–1883.

Macé, Albert. "La réforme des présidiaux au XVIIIᵉ siècle," *Bulletin de la Société polymathique du Morbihan,* 36 (1890): 127–137.

Mansergh, Martin. "The Revolution of 1771; or, The Exile of the Parlement of Paris." Ph.D. thesis, Oxford University, 1973.

Marion, Marcel. *Dictionnaire des institutions de la France aux XVIIᵉ et XVIIIᵉ siècles.* Paris: Picard, 1968.

——— *Le garde des sceaux Lamoignon et la réforme judiciaire de 1788.* Paris: Hachette, 1905.

Marquiset, Jean. *Les gens de justice dans la littérature.* Paris: Librairie Générale de Droit et de Jurisprudence, 1967.

Meyer, Jean. *La noblesse bretonne au XVIIIᵉ siècle.* Paris: Flammarion, 1972.

Michaud, Joseph. *Biographie universelle, ancienne et moderne.* 45 vols. New ed. Paris, 1842–1865.

Monnier, Francis. *Le Chancelier d'Aguesseau: Sa conduite et ses idées politiques et son influence sur le mouvement des esprits pendant la première moitié du XVIIIᵉ siècle.* Paris, 1860.

Mourant, John Arthur. *The Physiocratic Conception of Natural Law.* Chicago: University of Chicago Press, 1943.

Mousnier, Roland. *La vénalité des offices sous Henri IV et Louis XIII.* 2nd ed. Paris: Presses universitaires de France, 1971.

Nicholas, Barry. *An Introduction to Roman Law.* Oxford: Oxford University Press, 1962.

Pagé, Camille. *La coutellerie depuis l'origine jusqu'à nos jours.* 6 vols. Châtellerault, 1896–1904.

Parrine, Mary Jane. *Legal Reformism and Codification under Louis XIV: The Sense of Criminal Justice.* Ann Arbor: University Microfilms, 1974.

Perkins, Merle L. *The Moral and Political Philosophy of the Abbé de Saint-Pierre.* Geneva: Droz, 1959.

———— "Voltaire and the Abbé de Saint-Pierre," *The French Review,* 34 (1960): 152–163.

Piétri, François. *La réforme de l'état au XVIII' siècle.* Paris: Les Editions de France, 1935.

Pillot, Gabriel-Maximilien-Louis. *Histoire du Parlement de Flandres.* 2 vols. Douai, 1849–1850.

Richet, Denis. *La France moderne: L'esprit des institutions.* Paris: Flammarion, 1973.

Rogister, J. M. J. "Conflict and Harmony in Eighteenth-Century France: A Reappraisal of the Nature of the Relations between the Crown and the Parlement of Paris (1730–1754)." Ph.D. thesis, Oxford University, 1971.

Salmon, J. H. M. *Society in Crisis: France in the Sixteenth Century.* London: E. Benn, 1975.

Schneider, Mical H. *The French Magistracy,* 1560–1615. Ann Arbor: University Microfilms, 1974.

Seligman, Edmond. *La justice en France pendant la Révolution.* 2 vols. Paris: Plon-Nourrit, 1901–1913.

Smith, William, and Theophilus D. Hall. *A Copious and Critical English-Latin Dictionary.* New York, 1871.

Stone, Bailey Stillman. *Crisis in the Paris Parlement: The Grand'Chambriers, 1774–1789.* Ann Arbor: University Microfilms, 1973.

Thuillier, Guy. "Economie et administration au grand siècle: L'Abbé Claude Fleury," *La revue administrative,* 10 (1957): 348–357.

———— "Une 'utopie' au grand siècle: 'De la Réformation d'un Etat' de Géraud de Cordemoy (1668)," *La revue administrative,* 13 (1960): 257–262.

Tournerie, Jean-André. *Recherches sur la crise judiciaire en province à la fin de l'Ancien régime: Le Présidial de Tours de 1740 à 1790.* Tours: Faculté des Sciences juridiques et économiques, 1975.

Zeldin, Theodore. *France 1848-1945.* 2 vols. Oxford: Oxford University Press, 1973–1977.

# Index

Individual courts and other institutions are listed by their city or region.

# Harvard Historical Studies

85. *Patrice L. R. Higonnet.* Pont-de-Montvert: Social Structure and Politics in a French Village, 1700–1914. 1971.
86. *Paul G. Halpern.* The Mediterranean Naval Situation, 1908–1914. 1971.
87. *Robert E. Ruigh.* The Parliament of 1624: Politics and Foreign Policy. 1971.
88. *Angeliki E. Laiou.* Constantinople and the Latins: The Foreign Policy of Andronicus, 1282–1328. 1972.
89. *Donald Nugent.* Ecumenism in the Age of the Reformation: The Colloquy of Poissy. 1974.
90. *Robert A. McCaughey.* Josiah Quincy, 1772–1864: The Last Federalist. 1974.
91. *Sherman Kent.* The Election of 1827 in France. 1975.
92. *A. N. Galpern.* The Religions of the People in Sixteenth-Century Champagne. 1976.
93. *Robert G. Keith.* Conquest and Agrarian Change: The Emergence of the Hacienda System on the Peruvian Coast. 1976.
94. *Keith Hitchins.* Orthodoxy and Nationality: Andreiu Şaguna and the Rumanians of Transylvania, 1846–1873. 1977.
95. *A. R. Disney.* Twilight of the Pepper Empire: Portuguese Trade in Southwest India in the Early Seventeenth Century. 1978.
96. *Gregory D. Phillips.* The Diehards: Aristocratic Society and Politics in Edwardian England. 1979.
97. *Alan Kreider.* English Chantries: The Road to Dissolution. 1979.
98. *John Buckler.* The Theban Hegemony, 371–362 BC. 1980.
99. *John A. Carey.* Judicial Reform in France before the Revolution of 1789. 1981.